We Still Have

Questions

By

Bill L. Little, PhD

Table of Contents

Introduction: Asking Questions about Faith and God   Page

Chapter 1:   About God's Existence   6

Chapter 2:   An Early Question we ask   11

Chapter 3:   About Loving our Enemies   16

Chapter 4:   About the Meaning of Life?   22

Chapter 5:   About What Really Matters?   27

Chapter 6:   About Truth?   32

Chapter 7:   About Conflict between Science and Religion   37

Chapter 8:   About Church and Scriptures   40

Chapter 9:   About believing Every Word of the Bible as Literal & True   43

Chapter 10:   About Blending the Old and New Testaments   50

Chapter 11:   About the Influence of Jesus on Interpreting the Scripture   53

Chapter 12:   About Inconsistencies in the Bible   55

Chapter 13:   About the Best Thing we can do   59

Chapter 14:   About Answers to the Mysteries   61

Chapter 15:   About Jesus being Fully God and Fully Man   63

Chapter 16:   About what difference Prayer really makes   66

Chapter 17:   About What Heaven is like   69

Chapter 18:   About Right and Wrong Behavior   73

Chapter 19:   About sin   78

Chapter 20:   A Question about Death   81

Chapter 21:   Some questions we will continue to ask   84

Chapter 22:   The most important Question for me   88

Bibliography   93

We Still ask Questions

By

Bill L. Little

Introduction

Asking Questions about Faith and God are vital to seeking truth.

When we begin to ask questions about religion we are immediately under suspicion. So, we must examine our motives and aims when we raise questions about Christian faith. Our purpose in asking questions must be clear. We ask questions, not to argue points of view but to honestly seek answers in searching for truth.

Religion is the most important issue in my life and my faith in God is number one in areas of importance for me. It is too vital for me to ignore questions about that faith. I ask questions because I want to know the answers. I want to know truth and believe I must not be afraid to face questions that relate to this vital issue in my life. I want to know the truth.

There are certainly areas of religious faith that leave many people wondering about the validity of that faith. We must not fear facing their honest wondering in search for truth. The challenge we face is to ask the right questions from the best motives and do so in a respectful way. There is nothing, absolutely nothing wrong with asking questions in order to get answers about the important issues we face.

My father grew up on a farm and was only able to acquire a seventh grade education. In spite of his limitations he was able to become skilled in several different jobs and wound up his working life as a union electrician. When asked how he was able to learn so many different jobs he would raise his eyebrows and say, "Well, I was never too proud to say I didn't know how to do a thing and I was willing to ask questions about how to do things I couldn't do."

He told me on a number of occasions, "Never be afraid to ask questions for directions or how to do a job." I believe that is good advice for any of us to follow. So I have decided to write a manuscript on questions that I want to ask about religion and life.

Chapter 1

The question of God's existence

When I was about 10 years old, I asked my Dad where the moon, stars, and sun came from. He, almost nonchalantly, answered, "God created them."

I then asked him, "Well, where did God come from?"

He responded with more concern, "Bill, don't think about that too much. It can drive you crazy. I wouldn't ask that question anymore."

I did not ask him that question again but I have tried numerous times to seek an answer to it. I have found no definitive answer but I continue to believe in God.

My parents were not Christians but believed in God. I, however, spent a lot of my time as a young child with my Dad's parents. They were devout Christians and took me to church often. I basically grew up believing in God but not thinking very much about it. Still there were times when the thought about how God could exist came into my mind. I usually just dismissed it. I didn't want to go crazy.

As an adult my questions have continued, not so often about where God came from but, "How can we know that God exists?" I have continued to seek the answer to that because it was one of the most important questions in my life. Philosophers and theologians have offered ideas. Some of them help.

N.T. Wright (referenced in Collins book "Belief"), British theologian suggests that the seemingly innate awareness of right and justice within us are an indication of God's presence. He says that these ideas must come from somewhere and explaining that they came about as part of evolution does not explain them.

Any group of children on a playground seems to have an idea of what is just and right. You can hear "That's not fair" coming from their play. How do they know what is "fair"? We all seem to have an idea of what is right and just. I know that I do. I almost naturally know the difference between right and wrong and I am bothered by the fact that I often fail to do right and do wrong. There is something inside me that causes that concern. Is that God? I think so.

There are several philosophical arguments for the existence of God. I agree with a friend who is an engineer. He says philosophers should be called engineers because we are given impossible tasks with inadequate tools to achieve them. That may indeed be a good description of philosophy. Most of us find it difficult to understand. That does not keep us from trying because it so important. .

Aquinas was influenced a great deal by Aristotle in developing his "proofs" of God's existence. The idea that anything can come from nothing (ex-nihilo, Latin for "out of nothing") is impossible for us to comprehend. It is a philosophical concept that grows out of a faith that God created everything out of nothing. It is a matter of faith and while it is difficult for us to understand, as most philosophy is, it still offers us the only real arguments for the existence of God.

Listed below are five "proofs" of God's existence that at least can start us to thinking and give us clues to help begin to answer our questions about creation and God. I put quotation marks around "proof" because there is no way we actually prove the existence of God. We can however find strong evidence. This list comes from the book "Belief" by Francis Collins.

1. First, Aquinas says that there is motion. Motion exists, we can acknowledge that. He says that motion is caused. What causes motion? In trying to answer that question we begin to go back from one cause to another until we reach a cause that is immovable. It is motion that has no possible cause. He says that is where we find God...the unmoved mover.

I put a book on a table and left the room and when I came back the book was on a chair. I asked, "Who moved my book?" I was told that no one moved it. I just moved. I did not believe that answer. If the book was moved, someone or something moved it. We simply do not believe that things are set in motion with out an outside influence. Motion is an indication of a mover.

I can understand that concept and it offers me at least the beginning of a reason I can believe in God.

2. His second evidence for the existence of God is more difficult to understand. He finds what he calls "Efficient Causes." Efficient Cause is what brings about

change in things. His argument is that nothing can be its own cause for change. There must be a cause for the efficient causes that change things. He then says that nothing can be its own efficient cause because then it would have to exist before itself. That concept is mind boggling but somehow seems to make sense. His argument is that there must be a first Efficient Cause and that is where we find God.

3. Aquinas suggests that there exist possible and necessary things. I do not comprehend all that this means. Aquinas is saying that the things in the universe exist but there was a time when they did not exist so they could not come into existence from nothing (es nihilo) Then says there was a time when such things did not exist. There was a time when these things were not. Before they came to be there had to be a cause, something had to bring them into existence. I remember that in seminary we called this the existence of an "uncaused cause" and this is where we find God.

4. Fourth, there are some things that are "more" than others and "better" than others. A thing is said to be more or less as it approaches to that which is called most. He says, "Therefore exists something which is best and truest , the source of all thing best and truest." That is where we find God.

5. Fifth, he argues from the existence of government. Government brings together things that work together to achieve a desired goal. He says that even government cannot work together without being brought to the end by an outside force. This is not a clear argument for me but I can see that the outside force is where Aquinas finds God.

Some of these arguments are interesting and suggest the existence of God but I have trouble following the logic of all of them. Unmoved mover or uncaused cause makes the most sense to me. This may seem too simplistic for some but I continue to look for evidence. My search continues.

More convincing to me as an evidence of God's reality and presence in the world is the universal thirst and hunger for spiritual things. N. T. Wright (referenced in "Belief") returns to the possibility that "the widespread hunger for spirituality, which has been reported in various ways across the whole of human experience, is a genuine signpost to something that remains just around the corner, out of sight."

Hunger for spirituality may be the echo of a voice..."a voice that is calling, not so loudly as to compel us to listen whether we choose to or not, but not so quietly as to be drowned out altogether by the noises going on in our head and our world." Wright further notes, "If that voice were to join itself up with the passion for justice, some might conclude that it would at least be worth listening for further echoes of the same voice." The existence of that "voice" calling us to hunger for spiritual reality is a more compelling evidence for me that God is real and the author of that voice.

For me there are a couple of more clear "proofs" in the scriptures. The first is found in the Old Covenant book of Job. The primary value for me of the "old covenant" or Old Testament is in stories about courage and strength as well as some inspirational writings. This argument demonstrating the existence of God is one of those inspirational writings.

Job says, "...ask the animals, and they will teach you, or the birds of the air, and they will tell you, or speak to the earth, and it will teach you, or let the fish of the sea inform you. Which of all these does not know that the hand of the Lord has done this? (Job 12: 7-9)"

Paul makes a similar argument in Romans 1: 20 - 21. Here Paul appeals to the fact that God has made Himself known through His creation. He says, "For since the creation of the world God's invisible qualities—His eternal power and divine nature—have been clearly seen, being understood from what has been made, so that men are without excuse. For although they knew God, they neither clarified him as God nor gave thanks to him, but their thinking became futile and their foolish hearts were darkened."

Most conclude that there can be no absolute proof of God's existence but there are certainly a lot of things that suggest his existence. I believe that the presence of the moral law is one such evidence. The bottom line for me is that I believe in

God. My faith in God does not do away with my questions therefore I still have questions.

Chapter 2

An early question:

One of the first questions I learned to ask as a child was, "why?" "Why can't I go outside? Why can't I have candy? Why can't I go?" The most usual answer that I was given was "because I said so." Parents don't usually spend a lot of time explaining the "whys" that are voiced by children. Attempts at explaining why do not always really answer the question anyway.

A "why" question then that comes to my mind and that I am most often asked about faith in a loving God has to do with evil and suffering. Why does God allow evil and suffering?

As an adult I have continued to ask "why" on a number of occasions and I hear the questions raised by a lot of people. The usual question of why is worded, "why does God let bad things happen?" "Why do good people suffer?" The answers are not usually satisfying. "People do bad things and then bad things result." But the questions remain.

I was often told, "We will understand it someday." That never quenched my thirst for knowledge to know why." I still do not know the answer and wonder "Why". I have never been able to give a definitive answer to this question of why bad things happen but I have found some really helpful thoughts from some others who seek answers.

Francis Collins says that there are several answers to this dilemma. In general, he points out that at least part of the problem is that people have free wills. They can do what is right and best or not. He says, "Let us recognize that a large fraction of our suffering and that or our fellow human beings is brought about by what we do to one another." When a drunk driver hits and kills a young girl we can hardly blame God. When a stray bullet kills an innocent bystander we can hardly blame God. Human errors, bad judgment, and bad decisions cause human suffering.

Could this be stopped by God? C. S. Lewis says no. "If you choose to say 'God can give a creature free will and at the same time withhold free will from it,' you have not succeeded in saying anything about God…" Simply saying "God can" only adds to confusion. If He can, then why doesn't He? It seems that he doesn't withhold freewill and human beings still bring on pain and suffering by their free choices.

This answer can not be given by people who do not believe in "free will." If you believe that everything is predestined then the question "why" is simply answered "because God wanted it that way. That is not a satisfying answer for me. It is like the parents answer "because I said so."

I have learned not to "blame God" for the suffering and pain but that has not totally answered the question of "why" for me. It does move me a step closer to trusting God "no matter what happens." I believe God loves us and wants to help us learn and grow from the pain and suffering we may experience. It is certainly true that we do learn through suffering!

One of the least acceptable explanations for suffering is that it is brought on by sin. The question asked by the disciples about the reason a man was blind (John 9:1-5 "Who sinned this man or his parents?"

Jesus discounted the idea that was grounded in Old Covenant (Old Testament or Jewish Bible) concepts. He noted that suffering could even afford us the opportunity of demonstrating the power and comfort of God in helping suffering people to find support. The unfortunate idea was that if you did wrong you suffered and if you did right you were rewarded, often with material things or good health. It was not only a poor idea, adopted by prosperity gospel preachers. It was ridiculous.

Imagine this. If suffering came from doing wrong you could become a judge by simply checking to see if a person was healthy (doing right), or wealthy (also doing right) On the other hand if the person was suffering, unhealthy, or poor you could judge them as evil. That was the cause of suffering or poverty. As my ancestors used to say, "That old dog just won't hunt." Good health can come to evil people and poor health and suffering can come to very good people. Some of the best people I have ever known suffered. The idea is worse than ridiculous.

As a young pastor (age 23) I now know I was far too glib with my attempts to comfort suffering people, especially those who were experiencing severe grief. It wasn't until I lost some close family members and a couple of my closest friends that I learned real empathy (age 26).

I became a lot more empathic and that empathy grew over the years. I learned that there are no easy answers. My friend Don called me one night and told me that his wife and 4 year old son had been killed in a train/car collision. That was not long after my 26th birthday. Before that I had just lost one of my closest friends to a heart attack.

I met with Don. We literally wept together. I remember that he said to me, "Both of them, Bill. How can I make it?"

I said, "Don, sometimes all we can do is put one foot in front of the other and we do that through the tears." We sat for, what seemed to be an hour without saying anything else.

The next afternoon we went to the funeral home together. When we met he said something like, "Sometimes it is just hard to keep on putting one foot in front of the other." I just nodded. Two years earlier I would have been giving him some pretty pat answers to his losses but today it was much more real than any answers.

I have never again taken a loss through death lightly. I learned through my own pain when I nearly collapsed while walking in the funeral procession of one of my best friends. It is hard to give up people you love, no matter what your faith is.

I have said that part of the answer is that this is a fallen and evil world and things happen that are not in the will of God. How this can be reconciled with the power of a loving God, I do not know. I still believe in the love of God and trust that somehow the answers will come.

After a while I replaced the question of "why" with the questions, "what and how." To ask what does all this mean is one more difficult question?

I ask why bad things are happening and then ask "what can I or we do about any of it?" Part of that answer is "I can try to overcome pain caused by the presence of bad things in life. And I can stop doing bad things myself." This is a minimum of what I can do but even then I am faced with another question, "how."

I visited a church member's home one winter morning. When I arrived, I was led into a cold bedroom where there was no heat and a five year old child was sitting on a stool in the middle of the room. He was sobbing. Two other young children were in the room. They had also been crying.

The mother left the room and I went over to the child on the stool. "Don't move him." One of the children warned. "If he moves he will get another spanking."

When the mother returned I asked her what had happened. The child had an accident and spilled some water on the floor. The other children were in the room to learn a lesson about being careful.

I then discovered from her that this was typical punishment. It was obvious that the child was suffering needlessly. I tried to talk to her about him and she told me that when the father got home there would be more punishment.

I left wondering what I could do. How could I help those children? I decided to call Social Services and ask them to visit the home. Later that week they visited and discovered that the conditions were so bad and the parents so uncaring that they immediately removed the children and took them to a "children's home."

The parents were angry but made little effort to stop the process and the children were put into a home about 200 miles from St. Louis.

The children knew what I had done and three years later the oldest of them came to me at an event at the children's home where they had first been taken. She hugged me and said, "Thank you for getting us out of that home."

The problems in the home were really worse than I can describe. It was a second marriage for the mother and the step-father didn't want children any way. I am glad that I ran the risk of reporting the situation.

The more appropriate question is not, why is this suffering going on, but what can we do to make it better and how can we do that. If we ask the wrong questions we will never get the best answers.

I can understand how we learn from suffering. Nelson Mandela was transformed by his experience of being incarcerated for 27 years. The transformation moved him away from the anger he felt for the first few years. It enabled him to become a champion for reformation in South Africa. He learned compassion through his suffering.

I am still left with unanswered questions about the suffering of innocent children. That remains an area that really bothers me. I continue to look for answers.

We can learn from our own suffering and from the suffering of others. At least we will not compound the suffering if we pay attention and do what we can to make life better but we will still have questions.

Chapter 3

Can we really love and forgive our enemies?

Read Matthew 5:43-48. This passage begins "You have heard that it was said, You shall love you neighbor, and hate your enemy: but I say to you, Love your enemies, and pray for them that persecute you that you may be sons of your Father which is in heaven." Dietrich Bonhoeffer makes a point of the fact that this is the first time in the Sermon on the Mount that we see the word which sums up the whole message in that sermon. That word is "love."

The disciples were aware that they had "enemies." There were people who cursed them for following Jesus. They were accused of breaking the law and they did. They were accused of profaning the Sabbath, eating with 'unclean hands' and associating with sinners. This they also did. They had to regularly contend with hostility, mockery, and threats.

It must have been difficult for the disciples to hear that the way they were to overcome their enemies was to love them. It is hard to believe that Jesus is saying that we are to love our enemies, people who are hostile toward us. But that is what he said. We are then bound by His words. His words convey to us His will for us and that will is for us to love our enemies.

How are we to love? Obviously this cannot be an emotional response so it must be revealed as our action. How is love to behave? Jesus says, "Bless, do good and pray for your enemies without reserve and without respect of persons." Bonhoeffer says this is not a passive endurance of evil. "Here Jesus goes further and bids us not only to bear with evil and the evil person patiently, not only to refrain from treating him as he treats us, but actively to engage in heart-felt love towards him.

This commandment from Jesus rules out revenge. Most of us have had very little persecution and open hostility to face. The point is that we are to be prepared to face it when it comes. For me this is not a normal reaction to enemies and mistreatment but it is the way of Jesus. Jesus was a lot of things but "normal" was not one of them. He was extraordinary.

Bonhoeffer helped me to understand this "abnormal" reaction. The hallmark of the Christian life is the "extraordinary." We are to live the life that is described in the beatitudes. It is the way of self-renunciation, purity, meekness, and light. We are to live with love for our enemies, the kind of love that is exemplified by the cross.

The only possible way I can accomplish this is through the grace and presence of Jesus in my life. I have to rely on Him to live in me.

Perhaps we understand this command of Jesus is to begin with forgiveness. We are to forgive those who sin against us. That sounds difficult but it is worse than that. We don't understand it until we put it in context.

One writer told of how his daughter was held at knife point and raped. They never found the man who raped her but he and his daughter realized that the only way for them to really overcome this awful situation was to forgive the perpetrator and move forward with their lives. They both did that and both became active in helping others deal with tragic situations in their lives.

I have read of parents who openly forgave people who have murdered their children. That is a step closer to loving them than most of us can even imagine going and forgiving is one thing but loving?

It is easy to talk about forgiveness until someone hurts you or, even more, when they hurt someone you love. For me it is even broader than that. I have trouble feeling forgiveness toward people who hurt weaker people, the underdogs.

I believe that we can forgive if we understand how much we have been forgiven and how much we need forgiveness ourselves. I hope I have the wisdom and the grace to be forgiving and tender heart ed toward others. God has certainly been all of that and more to me.

I think a lot about forgiveness and believe it is absolutely essential in order to live the Christian life. That is stated in many ways and often in the New Testament.

Forgiveness is a multifaceted thing. It touches us in many different ways...when we need to be forgiven, when we need to forgive, and when we feel forgiven. We may never forget the things that hurt us but we can stop holding them against those who hurt us. The forgiveness of God restores a right relationship with Him and fills the emptiness in my life. It calms my fears. After failures in my life, nothing in the world is sweeter than the forgiveness of God and restoration to Him in a loving relationship.

It is not an easy thing to forgive as Paul instructed the Corinthians. When one repents and is forgiven the forgiveness is not complete until that one is restored to love in the fellowship of Christ. Forgiveness is not complete until restoration is made.

When a marriage experiences unfaithfulness of one spouse and the other still would like to save the marriage this can happen. It can happen if the guilty spouse honestly repents and wants to work on saving the marriage. That may sound like enough but it is not. If the "forgiving" spouse has the attitude "I will forgive you but I'll never trust you again" the marriage is not likely to be saved.

Forgiveness is not complete until there is restoration. Both members must want to work together to restore their trust and love. Then and only then are they assured that the marriage can survive and become whole again. Restoration is an essential part of forgiveness.

I have questions about forgiveness. I have been taught, and I believe it is true, that we are to forgive one another in the same way we have been forgiven. Most of us have trouble with this concept and certainly with this action. The question for us is, "How can we become more forgiving to others?" Another question, just as significant is, "How can we become more forgiving of ourselves?"

I have had little and no experience with the kind pain inflicted by those who rape and murder. I have however dealt with someone who felt hurt by me and then went out of his way to find ways to hurt me. I asked for his forgiveness but he continued his assault on my life and tried to destroy everything that was meaningful to me.

My first reactions to this man were anything but love. I had to take it one step at a time. I began by praying for him. I didn't want to pray for him but felt that it was the right thing to do. It did not occur to me at first that I needed to love him. I just prayed for him...every day.

The praying became easier and after a while I felt comfortable praying for him and then felt good about praying for him. I began to think of him as really struggling with his own feelings of hurt. I began to empathize and then to experience some warmth for him. I continued to pray for him and believe this is what it takes to love him.

The point for me is that loving may be a step by step process that begins with acting in the right way (praying for) and continues to grow into warm emotional feelings. For Jesus it was not a step by step process. He simply loved His enemies. I admire that in Him and want to obey His commands.

I don't like the idea of loving my enemies (anyone who seeks to hurt me or my friends and family) but I believe that is what I am supposed to do. I want to do it because it is what the love of Jesus demands of me.

Probably an important point is to remember that we cannot love unless we can forgive and we must forgive if we are to obey the teachings of Jesus. But how often are we to forgive. That question was put to Jesus by the disciples and his answer was "to seven times seventy." We are to forgive until forgiveness becomes a quality of our lives. As hard as that may be to accept I want to accept it because I need forgiveness in my life...over and over again.

A point that often is left out of discussions on forgiveness is the need we have to forgive ourselves. When we recognize our sins, confess them, and repent of them God forgives us. Still we often have trouble forgiving ourselves. The truth is that I have trouble or even find it impossible to forgive others if I cannot forgive myself of similar problems.

I have committed many sins, some of them are blatant. I have confessed, repented, and asked God for forgiveness. Still I live with regrets and guilt because of those sins in my life. I cannot undo them. I cannot change them. I can only forgive them. I tell myself that I can forgive those sins if I see them in others but have trouble forgiving them in me.

My oldest son, a supervising attorney for JAG, has helped me to understand the importance of self forgiveness. He said, "If I don't forgive myself, I will have trouble forgiving my clients of similar errors in their lives. That makes it difficult, if not impossible, to give them a competent representation in court."

One thing that helps me to take that step of self forgiveness is to commit clearly to not ever committing those sins again. If I do that, I can forgive myself and then am free to forgive others of similar sins. It is also a part of self forgiveness to begin to treat myself as if I have been forgiven. Reject the guilt and remind myself that "I am a forgiven child of God. I am thankful for that." With that I can lift my head and look squarely at the world.

An example would be when I hear of a professional person committing sexual sins I remember that I have committed those same sins. If I cannot forgive myself I will find it impossible to forgive others. On the other hand, if I forgive myself, I can honestly, with congruence forgive others for the same and even different sins. The key is that I must be able to accept God's grace for me before I can clearly express it for others.

My point in sharing this is that I want others to know that if they are struggling with guilt over past sins I want to be an instrument of God in expressing forgiveness to them. That includes wanting to restore them to a right relationship with God and others.

Still the outstanding example of forgiveness in my mind is the account of Jesus praying that God would forgive those who were crucifying Him. Knowing the example and His call upon us to forgive one another as He has forgiven us really challenges us to let Him forgive through us.

I think that the most challenging statement about love and forgiveness is made by Jesus when he adds "as I have..." He says love one another as I have loved you. The lesson is clear. Forgive one another as I have forgiven you. It is tough enough to love and forgive others without being challenged to love and forgive as Jesus did.

If we all learned to love and forgive as Jesus loved and forgave problems in the world would begin to disappear. Certainly, if we Christians practiced loving one another as Jesus loved and loves us, church fellowships would become magnetic.

.

Chapter 4

Another important question is "What is the meaning of life?"

It would be hard to overemphasize the importance of this question. The loss of meaning is a destructive experience. It is too often experienced by retired people but it can come to anyone who forgets that life has purpose and it is not just life but <u>my</u> life that has purpose.

To find meaning, we will have to go beyond the scope of science and ask for how to find meaning by looking at religious sources. The search takes us to prison camps and philosophy as well as to religious works.

I still go back to read Viktor Frankl's book "Man's Search for Meaning." It is a powerful book written by a man who went through extended prison camp experience in Germany during World War II. He relied heavily on words from Nietzsche, "He who has a 'why' to live for can bear almost any 'how.'"

Frankl's book has been a painful one for me to read because I have read so much about the author's experience in those prison camps. Though he suffered immense pain, he learned powerful lessons from the experiences. Frankl says that he could see that people who had a task waiting for them were more likely to survive than those who had no sense of purpose.

His book and story took on tremendous significance for me when my wife and I visited the prison camp where he was held captive. I walked among the beds where the prisoners slept. They had no room to turn over and had to sleep on one side but they made it. I felt their presence when I placed my hand on the side of the bed where some of them slept. It brought to life for me how much Frankl suffered and how resolute he was in making it through. He did!

He had a purpose. He was working on a manuscript for a book when he was captured and put into a concentration camp. He tried to hide the manuscript in his coat but the coat and manuscript were taken from him and destroyed. It became his purpose to live and rewrite that manuscript.

He survived against all odds and "Man's Search for Meaning" was the result of his survival.

That book has paved the way for many to seek meaning and purpose in their lives. He says in his work that the most serious mental problem people are facing is the loss of meaning. Therapists are urged to help people find meaning in their lives. If we are not able to find meaning we will become bored, depressed, discouraged, and will lose energy and passion for living fully. Finding meaning for life drives me to look for the things that matter. Things that matter can fill our lives with meaning.

Meaning and purpose are closely connected. There are things we can do that no one else can do in our place. Some of these things relate to our families. Some of them relate to projects we have started and count as important.

I have no idea if anyone will ever read my thoughts as recorded in this manuscript but I have started this project and it gives me a sense of purpose to continue pursuing writing. It is at least part of my purpose for today. It gives me energy to keep pursuing it.

Life becomes meaningful when we begin to find significance in many of the moments of our days. We can discover meaning in a lot more of life than we think. We just have to decide how important it is for us to live meaningfully.

Not everything that we do has meaning in the deepest sense of that word. A lot of things are necessarily just routine and common place. Still the attitude with which we do those things can add significance to them.

I love the little book by Brother Lawrence, "Practicing the Presence of God." This monk made his life meaningful by practicing the presence of God in all that he did. When he washed dishes, he prayed that God would cleanse him as he cleansed the dishes. Whatever his daily tasks, he practiced focusing on the presence of God in those tasks. That made them meaningful for him.

Again, I am not suggesting that we find purpose in everything that we do but we can find a lot more when we become focused on finding it. I don't see much meaning in picking up trash beside the highway. But I have a friend in Arizona who decided to make his morning walk a time to help clean the highway. He picked up trash and had a sense of making the world a cleaner place by doing that. It was a small thing but if enough small things are done they can become significant for us.

It is my hope that by drawing attention to the desire for meaning in life we will grow in our ability to discover more of it for ourselves.

A lot of this will have to do with our focus. Much of life is determined by focus. We can live happier and healthier lives if we learn to focus on the positive things around us and learn to see the good and beautiful in people. We will be unhappy and unhealthy if we focus on the negative and ugly things around us.

I believe it is true that the result of focus is determined, not by external reality but by our internal interpretations of reality. The world is not as it is but as I see it to be. This is the reason that two people can see and hear the same things but interpret them in totally different ways.

The ability to find meaning in daily living is determined by the habits we have formed by our focus. Most people would like to experience more meaning in life and we can, if we develop the habit of watching for it. The material I have written in this book is designed to help us become more conscious of the many ways we can find meaning in life.

I believe that my life has meaning but it has more meaning when I recognize that there is meaning possible for all the people around me. My life has more meaning if I can help others find meaning for their lives.

When I practice loving other people enough to help them find meaning I will certainly find more purpose for myself. It is in forgetting about self and beginning to help others find meaning for their lives that I discover what is best for me. In other words, when I die to myself and live for others I will reach a new dimension for my life as well.

I met and talked to a man today. He is less than half my age. He is presently out of work and has no career. He is having trouble feeling that his life has meaning. I cannot get him out of my mind. I keep trying to think of ways I might be able to help him find work that is appropriate for him.

An interesting thing happened to me when I left him today. I felt more energized than I have felt in weeks. I know it was because my focus had shifted from myself to him. I am focused on trying to help him find meaning and it seems that in that pursuit I am inadvertently finding more meaning for myself.

It seems to me that a lot of what I see as having meaning in my life has been discovered in retrospect. It makes it seem almost accidental. Most of my life has been lived like that. I seldom sat down and asked, "Now what would give meaning to my life today?"'

I usually discovered the meaning, if there was any, by looking back. In addition to that, I have found that a lot of my life would start in one direction and then situations would necessitate a change of direction. It makes me wonder about "choosing" to live with purpose and meaning.

When I was choosing a direction for my PhD dissertation I decided to study what makes marriages fail or succeed. I began collecting data to find the characteristics of "successful' marriage. After more than two years of research, the chairman of the human research committee determined that I could not continue looking a marriage. He said something about the possibility that I might cause the couple to think of something that was wrong that they had not thought about.

I never understood but dropped the study and decided to study counseling techniques that might help cancer patients fight cancer and win. That resulted in a six-year study working with cancer patients at a radiation unit of a local hospital. Seven years from the beginning of that project my second book was published on "How to Fight for your Life." That has been rewritten to "Eight Ways to take an Active Role in Your Health." That book brought perceived meaning to my life.

Did I begin to search for meaning and find it in a book? No. I was almost forced into the study in order to finish my degree.

In that whole process a professor who taught marriage and family therapy at the university I was attending heard about my original study on marriage. He asked me to share that study with his class. He liked what I had found and asked me to substitute for him when he became ill. When he died I inherited his class.

When a local radio station called the university to find an "expert" in family therapy to do a program for them it was decided that that would be the teacher of the marriage and family therapy class. That was a class that I had inherited.

I did the radio program and that evolved into more than ten years of doing a regular call-in radio program. I found meaning again in doing something that I had not planned.

Again and again I have found that meaning came into my life more by circumstance than by choice. I sometimes believe that God was "guiding my life." I can accept that by faith but I cannot claim that I found meaning by my search. So, how can I find meaning now? Probably by learning to focus on what is going on around me and to me. When I look for the guidance of God I am likely to find it.

It is in helping others and becoming less selfish that we discover energy and passion for living. I don't want to forget that. I have calls to make this week and I hope that by the time I finish writing this manuscript I will be able to help some of the people I visit to find new meaning for life.

How many people in your life need some help in finding direction? It would be an act of love, if you could help them find purpose for themselves. I believe that matters. This is one thing that can become meaningful for all of us. But I still have a lot of questions about it.

Chapter 5

This leads to the question then *"So what really matters?"*

After asking this question, I came across the book "What Matters Most" by Karen Wyatt. That book has influenced my thinking. It is a book that describes lessons for living learned from stories of the dying. In this work, Dr. Wyatt lists 7 lessons learned from stories of the dying. I have found it to be challenging and helpful.

Lesson one relates to suffering. She says that she learned from dying patients to "Embrace Your Difficulties." When we embrace our suffering we learn that it is one of the things that connects us to all others. Everyone suffers and when we learn to accept it and learn from it to help others ease their suffering we usually discover that we ease our own pain.

A second lesson is the lesson of "love." When we love we will find our hearts being broken. That is one price for living with love. Love is essential for living with meaning.

There are several valuable lessons on discovering the things that matter but the one that sticks with me most is the lesson of impermanence. Since nothing in this world is permanent, certainly not our lives or belongings, then we learn not to seek meaning in the things in this world. Not our collections but our connections matter. That concept helps me to place value, not on things but on spiritual truth and people.

This seems to me to be a vital question to answer every day. Am I seeking things that really matter? You might be surprised at the results of a survey reported by Viktor Frankl. 7,948 students at forty-eight colleges participated in a survey done by social students at Johns Hopkins University. This was a part of a two year study sponsored by the National Institute of Mental Health.

When students were asked what they considered "very important" to them, 16 percent checked "making a lot of money." The only thing surprising about that is the small percentage. More surprising was that 78 percent said their first goal was finding a purpose and meaning for life.

It appears that most people realize that we need something for the sake of which we want to live. One of the things that seems to matter is finding a purpose for which to live. As indicated in the previous chapter, the loss of purpose and meaning is powerfully damaging to the levels of energy and passion we have for life.

What are some of the things that matter according to the New Testament? There are clearly powerful passages that clarify the things that matter. I turn here to find answers that science can never give me. I am not demeaning the value of science but I believe that religion, especially the religion of the New Testament guides us to the things that really matter most. This answers a very important question for us. What things matter enough for me to live my life in the pursuit of them?

Matthew 25 lists things that matter according to the teachings of Jesus. Read that chapter and note the things that mattered to Him. Feeding hungry people, visiting prisoners, clothing the naked, and caring for the sick are examples of what things mattered to Jesus. Involving ourselves in any of those activities will matter.

Matthew 5: 3-11 gives a list of characteristics that matter in this passage that we know as the Beatitudes. Reading this list will reveal to us characteristics like humility, meekness, righteousness, mercy, and peacemaking that certainly matter.

Look then at the 5th chapter of Galatians, verses 22-26 and read there the "fruit of the Spirit." Love, joy, peace, patience, kindness, goodness, faithfulness, gentleness, and self-control are all listed here. It seems obvious that these things matter.

I believe that standing up for people who need help really matters. I was in Boy Scout camp many (many) years ago when I saw a little guy being pushed around by a much bigger guy. I intervened and stepped between them. It didn't seem like much but it mattered to the little guy.

I saw that little fellow twenty five years later at a high school class reunion. He came up to me and told me how much it meant to him when I stepped between him and the boy who was pushing him around. He said, "I will never forget you for helping me."

About ten years later I was at another class reunion and was approached by the widow of the "boy" I had helped. She told me that he had died two years earlier but that even at the time of his death he remembered what I had done for him.

The point here is that though it was a small thing it mattered to him. If we can find things that matter to others and help them in those ways it matters for us as well. As in seeking meaning, looking for things that matter does not involve seeking dramatic or "big" things.

Helping lost people find their way matters. When we think we see someone who has lost his/her way or seem afraid we can ask him/her if they need help. If they do we can help them. It is as simple as that and that matters.

Doing things that matter not only helps others. It helps us. I always feel better about myself when I believe I have done something that has made a positive contribution to someone's life.

Jesus says that the greatest commandment involves loving God with all our hearts and minds and souls and then to love our neighbor as we love ourselves. He further says that doing unto others as we would have them do unto us is a summary of the law and the prophets.

The Apostle Paul picks up this in 1 Corinthians 13 where he proclaims that love is the greatest of all attributes of those who seek to serve God. In fact, Paul says that if we observe all other commands and even give our bodies as martyrs, if we do not have love...all the rest of these things amount to nothing.

I believe it is vital to ultimate satisfaction in life to sort out the lesser things and embrace the major things. The following quote puts it into perspective for me. I came across it in a book titled "Life Matters." It comes from Harry Emerson Fosdick and he wrote it in 1923. Give a look.

"There are more things to do than we ever shall get done; there are more books to read than we ever can look at; there are more avenues to enjoyment than we ever shall find time to travel. Life appeals to us from innumerable directions crying 'Attend to me here!' In consequence, we litter our lives with indiscriminate preoccupation. We let first come be first served, forgetting that the finest things do not crowd. We let the loudest voices fill our ears, forgetting that asses bray, but gentlemen speak low. Multitudes are living, not bad but frittered lives---split, scattered, uncoordinated. They are like pictures into which a would-be artist has put, in messy disarray, everything he has chanced to see; like music into which has been hurled "helter-skelter" every vagrant melody that has strayed into the composer's mind. Preoccupation is the most common form of failure." ("Twelve Tests of Character")

That may be why Lin Yutang (Chinese author and philosopher) said, "The wisdom of life consists in the elimination of non-essentials." At the very least we would be wise to prioritize the things that occupy our attention and time in life and eliminate some of the things that really do not matter.

To say that God matters is not the same as saying that religion matters. Not all religion matters if we mean by religion rituals consisting of formal worship and orthodox creeds, then much of it does not matter. **Unless we are made into better people from the rituals, doctrines, and worship in religion it is of no real value to us.** A lot of what is practiced as religious doesn't matter much at all.

A story was made up about people standing in a line to enter the gates of heaven. At one point a man was seen running and leaping with joy when someone in the line asked what was making him so happy. He must have been a Baptist because he said, "They are telling us at the gate that Wednesday night church attendance doesn't count." A lot of what we call religious practice probably doesn't count.

A lot of people are not going to believe this but I believe that who we are means a lot more than what we believe. Your theology can be as straight as a gun barrel and your life can be just as empty as that gun barrel. Real faith in Jesus produces lives grounded in love, compassion, respect, forgiveness, peace, joy, and service. Our attitudes matter more than our orthodoxy. Our commitment to Christ matters far above our organized religion or denomination. Read Matthew 25 again.

So what kind of religion does matter? I believe it is religion that focuses on respect, reverence, and acceptance of and for one another. That is religion that results in service and it grows out of our faith in God. It grows out of our awareness of God. (More about what matters in religion is covered in Chapter 9.)

God matters so much that we would be wise to think about Him as often as possible every day. In his book "Life the Game with Minutes" Frank Luabach says that we win every minute that we think about God. I thought this so important that I wrote a devotional book for members of our church that I called, "How to Think About God Every Day." Brother Lawrence's classic book, "Practicing the Presence of God" gives us guidance for filling our days with an awareness of God. He thought about God when he was washing dishes and doing other daily tasks.

For those of us who believe in God we can acknowledge two things. Either God matters or He does not matter. Not all who believe in God really act like He matters at all. When we accept the fact that God matters we can then begin to more clearly see the other things that matter or don't matter. Not only does God matter, He matters more than anything else in the world and in our lives.

Not only does God matter, what we believe about God matters as well. Jesus revealed God as father who loves His children and wants us to love one another. First John states it clearly, "God is love" (chapter 4:8). God is love and a lot more but if we believe in God as He is revealed in Jesus then we have the ideal place to begin looking at things that actually matter and those that do not matter.

Things that matter should become our foundation. When God is the foundation of our value system we have built on the rock but other foundations are like sand. Those buildings simply will not stand the test of life's demands. Those buildings will crash when the storms of life come (Matthew 7: 24-28). Build on the Rock.

Most of what matters in life for me is a matter of faith. I believe what matters is what Jesus taught and I want to build on that but I still have a lot of questions.

Chapter 6

Another important question: "What is Truth?"

Jesus said that "You shall know the truth and the truth will set you free" (John 8:32). While I believe that, I still find myself asking with Pontius Pilate, "What is truth?"

Truth and facts get tangled up. They are not the same thing. I have learned that facts, or perceived facts, change. There are many examples of that. For instance there was a time when it was a fact that the world was flat. That fact has changed. When the facts change then truth is more likely to appear.

For many years the fact was that the earth was the center of this solar system. At least that was the "perceived" fact. The leaders of the church believed that and defended it as "the way it was." The sun rose in the morning and set in the evening and that was a day. Then came scientists saying "wait a minute. The earth is not the center, the sun is." That was truth but it could not be easily accepted because it didn't fit with the "facts."

When scientists insisted, they were excommunicated or executed by the church. Then after fruitless resistance, the truth prevailed. Still we say the sun rises and sets but we understand that the sun is at the center and the earth rotates around it and that is the truth.

I remember when the first attempts were being made to land a man on the moon. I had an uncle who knew that wouldn't happen because he knew the facts and the facts indicated that we would never be able to land a man on the moon.

In a brief period of time the perception of those facts was changed and a man landed on the moon. My uncle, along with many others who clung to the "facts" did not believe the truth. They thought we were all being duped by made up video. I believe my uncle died clinging to "the facts."

Truth trumped facts, again.

Jesus told stories to help us understand truth and he didn't worry about "facts" in the stories. He told about a man who had a two by four in his eye judging another who had a speck in his eye. We know it was just a story and that no one ever really had a two by four sticking out of his eye but we also know that Jesus was telling us a truth. The truth is that we often are blinded by our own sins while judging the sins of others.

Stories are used throughout the Bible to reveal truth. Literalists are often so blinded by "facts" that they cannot see the truth that is being revealed. When we become overly concerned about our "facts" we hinder the discovery of truth.

Was Jonah really swallowed by a big fish and later coughed up on the shore? Are those facts or they just part of a story that is meant to reveal truth to us? The truth is that we are to share the message of God's redeeming love with people even if we don't like those people. That is the truth of the story of Jonah.

Was the world really created in 7 actual human timed days? What are the facts? There are two different sets of facts in Genesis one and two. In Genesis one animals were created and then man. In Genesis two man was said to have been created first and then named the animals. That doesn't bother me. Those facts don't measure up but they still reveal the vital truth. "God created the world." That is the truth.

As long as people of the church cling to their "facts" and resist truth that is revealed through science then people of science will not listen to the truth that we believe. Science can tell us "how" but faith can tell us "why." We certainly benefit when we bring the two together.

Truth is not just in what we say. It is in what we do. Jesus taught that we are to live by the truth and come into the light of God (John 3: 21). We are to worship in spirit and truth (John 4: 23 -24).

Truth is important because we build faith on it and often plan our lives around it.

Truth is important because it frees us in our memory. My dad and I were at a family reunion in Mississippi when some of our relatives started laughing at him and telling me about the time he drove over half way down to the reunion and turned around because it was too far. They said he went back home.

On our trip back home I asked him why he did that. He said, "Did what?" I said, "Drive over half way down to the reunion and turn around and go home because it was too far to drive."

He said that he hadn't done that. So I asked him why he didn't tell them that he hadn't done that. He said, "Because last year I might have told them that I did."

When you tell the truth it improves your memory.

But a more important reason for telling the truth is that it builds trust and respects others. It is what the love of Jesus demands of us.

So what is truth? One answer is "truth is that which is ultimately, finally, and absolutely real, or the 'way it is,' and therefore utterly trustworthy and dependable, being grounded and anchored in God's own reality and truthfulness." ("Belief" page 78) Christians invite people to put their faith in God because the message about God is true. Truth is true, not because I hope it is, not because I feel like it is, not because I want it to be but because it simply is true. Truth is true independent of any human "knower". It is true because it is objective and independent of the minds of people.

Truth is not created by us but discovered by us. For me that is an "aha" moment. There are times when truth really hits us. It may be something that we have "known" for a long time but suddenly it becomes our truth.

This is a mundane illustration but it is honest. For almost a year after my graduation from college, I was told "You are gaining weight." I said, "I know, I know."

That was an exchange that went on for a couple of months then at the end of winter, I tried to put on last year's trousers. I couldn't fasten the button on the waste. I stood in from of the mirror and exclaimed, "I am gaining weight!, I am becoming fat!" That was a moment of truth for me. I discovered it.

I call it an "existential moment." We have moments like that and they are really important when they come to us in reference to things that really matter. I hope for many moments like that in relationship to God. I have had a few moments when it "hit" me that God is real. It is true.

One author, L'Engle. noted that what human truth claims may be relative because humans are finite. But "truth is God's truth and is true everywhere, for everyone, under all conditions. It is created by God, not by us. It is partly discovered and partly disclosed. It is 'truth' singular. It is certain, not doubtful, absolute and unconditional, not relative, and it is grounded in God's infinite knowing.

Living in "truth" means being who we claim to be. It demands honesty. That honesty frees us from the stress of pretense. Being true to our faith is vital to emotional and spiritual health.

As Os Guinness (Author and cultural critic) says, "...truth matters infinitely and ultimately because it is a question of the trustworthiness of God himself." We may not always like the truth that we discover as God's reality but it is truth that we must not fear. Search for truth and accept it for what it is.

Madeleine L'Engle (author of "A Wrinkle in time) says that the world, especially the Christian world, is hung up on "literalism" and therefore confuses truth and fact. There are Christians who base their beliefs solely on the Bible. "The Bible is not objective. Its stories are passionate, searching for truth (rather than fact), and searching most deeply in story." L'Engle says that when she was researching the Bible for a book she was writing she discovered "more contradictions than she had remembered...two different ways of bringing David himself into the story, two different versions of Saul's death.." are examples.

She concludes that what the biblical narrative is trying to do is to tell the truth about King David and the truth is more important than facts. We don't need faith for facts but we do need faith for truth. The Bible does not demand of us that we take it all literally. Just study and search for truth. We, Christians are not saved because we believe every word of the Bible literally but because we believe in Jesus.

People who base their faith on what is written in the Bible will ultimately run into contradictions and stories that will threaten their faith. The first believers in the resurrection of Jesus did not have a Bible. They knew the story and told it as truth leading hundreds of people to faith in Christ before the Bible came into existence.

Truth is truth, not because it is written in the Bible but because it is truth. Paul could never have become a Christian if he had to find truth in the Bible. **He had no Bible** but he met Jesus on the road to Damascus. That was where he discovered truth.

For Christians the truth is based on the resurrection story and the Damascus road experience of Paul as he recorded it in the New Testament. That truth is vital and it is a lot more than facts or a literal interpretation of scripture.

Chapter 7

There is a question about the conflict between science and religion: This is a recurring question for serious believers.

Some will think that many of these questions should not be asked because they seem to question faith in and the authority of the scriptures. I contend that we should never be reluctant to ask questions that we have about faith and religion because of the importance the answers have for us. I do not intend these questions to be arguments but I believe they are valid and can be asked sincerely in a positive spirit.

I can remember asking questions when I was in seminary and being told by some of my friends that I shouldn't ask those questions but simply accept matters of religion by faith. An early example would be questions about creation. I would ask how could there be such a difference between the idea that the world was created in seven days and the idea promoted by science that the world was millions, if not billions of years old. I simply could not ignore the scientific evidence without questioning.

The most profound answer to the question about the conflict between religion and science that I have found was written by Francis Collins in his book "The Language of God." He said that science deals with the realm of nature and religion deals with the realm of the spiritual. Science attempts to answer the questions about "how" and religion attempts to answer questions about "why." We need to learn to wrap our minds around both and embrace them as valid.

This is a vital paragraph from Collin's book.

"Science is the only reliable way to understand the natural world and its tools when properly utilized can generate profound insights into material existence. But science is powerless to answer questions such as 'Why did the universe come into being?' 'What is the meaning of human existence?' 'What happens after we die?' One of the strongest desires of humankind is to seek answers to profound questions and we need to bring the power of both the scientific and the spiritual perspectives to bear on understanding what is both seen and unseen." We can integrate both areas.

It seems to me that rejecting discoveries of science because they don't line up with our preconceived notions about religious faith is one way to turn people away from religious faith. The temptation of too many religious people is to try to rationalize away scientific discoveries. That is usually a fruitless endeavor.

It is also a mistake for scientists to try to incorporate religion into science. Scottish evangelist Henry Drumond made that mistake in the 1800's . He tried to blend scientific evolution and spiritual evolution. The two are separate fields and should be left as separate. I look to science to tell me about how things work in the natural world. When we do not view science as a threat to faith we can learn a lot about the world that God created.

Scientists are also missing a lot when they ignore the insight of spiritual minds into the meaning of the world.   Closed minds in either science or religion can do nothing to advance the interests of the other.

These are important things to remember when we explore scientific theories of evolution. Certainly we can accept these theories as probably true without violating our desire to search for meaning in life.

Andy Stanley (Atlanta Pastor and best-selling author) writes some powerful observations about what happens when we are able to remove some of the barriers that have been thrown up between believers and science. He says, "It's remarkable what happens when people don't feel like they have to choose between science and Christianity....It's remarkable what happens when a high school student realizes the creation story is not the make or break for her faith."

He goes on to say "It's remarkable what happens when thoughtful Christians who for years harbored secret doubts and questions discover that the foundation of their faith is not an inerrant text or non-contradicting Gospels. It's remarkable what happens when college freshmen discover that the violence and unsubstantiated historical references in the Old Testament don't undermine the message of Jesus. It's remarkable what happens when a biology major discovers his Christian faith doesn't teeter on the brink of irrelevance based on how long it took the universe to form."

He further points out that we can accept the message of Jesus without having to believe a man put two of every kind of animal on a boat and then see God flood the world and kill everyone except that man and his family. We have certainly put too many barriers blocking honest seekers from accepting Jesus Christ.

Eventually I would conclude that the world came into existence through evolution that took billions of years. I concluded it was enough for me to affirm my faith that God was behind it all, no matter how long it took or how it was done. This was just one of the questions that I had been told not to ask. Conservative Christian friends strongly suggested to me that this question was inappropriate.

Over the past few months I have concluded that there are a lot of questions that can and should be asked about the things we believe. Not all of the questions originated in my mind but I have accepted them as valid questions. I hope we are beyond the place that questions threaten or offend us. The issues are too important to leave without challenging them with honest and valid questions.

Chapter 8

A vital question about the church and the scriptures:

One question that has been helpful for me in my desire to understand the church and its relationship to the scriptures is one that I believe I read in the writings of Andy Stanley. It is "Did the scriptures create the church or did the church create the scriptures?"

The answer seems pretty simple. The church was in existence at least three hundred years before the existence of the Bible. The Bible is a compilation of writings from the Jews and early Christians. The Hebrew Scriptures coupled with the writings of the early disciples formed the history and theology that led to the Bible.

Note that these were collected and compiled by Christian groups meeting, debating, and voting on what to include in the Bible. This process was followed by early Christians who put together the scriptures into what we have as our Bible. The church predates the existence of the Bible and thus had to influence and gather its content.

The Gospels were written and all the letters of apostles (including the apostle Paul) were in existence before the Bible was compiled no earlier than 300AD.

We probably need a clearer concept of "church." Church is certainly a lot more and different from an organized group of people meeting in a building called church. It seems that the earliest idea about church was a group of people who bound themselves together around the belief that Jesus is the Son of God who was crucified for our sins and raised from the dead by the power of God.

It was not always easy to find "believers" in the early years of the "church." It became much easier when regular meeting places were found, in homes, in market places, in warehouses, even in the catacombs. Little by little that evolved into special buildings (churches).

Why is this important? For me it is important because when I read the Bible I know I am reading the history of the actions of the apostles and their ideas as they began the church long before it became the church. I know that there were summaries of ideas that influenced the theology of the church. What they thought or believed became the theology of the church.

Some of these ideas were adopted as the "word of God." You will hear people appealing to authority saying, "The Bible says..." Actually the Bible doesn't "say" anything. It is a book that quotes what many people have said. Paul says, Jesus says, Peter says, or even Moses says may be accurate but the Bible didn't say these things, the men named said them and they are recorded in the Bible. That makes a big difference when appealing to authority.

We are challenged to always be prepared to give an account to everyone who asks why we have hope in Jesus. Nowhere have I read that we are to be ready to give an account of why we believe the scriptures are without error. Our hope is not in an inerrant book but in a living Lord, Jesus Christ. He is our hope.

The source of my faith in Jesus as Savior was first from my grandmother's testimony and example. That faith was verified and strengthened by the testimonies of Matthew, Mark, Luke, John, and Paul. I trust their testimonies as recorded in the New Testament. The fact that there are inconsistencies in the writing does not remove the validity of their testimonies.

The church (people who believe in Jesus) created the Bible. This is vital to being able to understand and find answers to other questions about such things as women's role in the church and attitudes we have toward such issues as social drinking, divorced people serving in the church, among other issues that will follow.

Christians make a mistake when we try to make the Old Testament (Or Old Covenant) speak to the teachings of the Jews on how we should live. Jesus gave us a new way of approaching faith. Read Hebrews chapter 7. This new way given to us by Jesus is better than the old way. ("...Jesus has become the guarantee of a better covenant verse 22). He is our high priest forever.

We can easily rationalize the use of Old Covenant thoughts in teaching about Jesus. We say that at least there is prophecy that tells us a Messiah is coming and describes some of His attributes. Many of the prophecies we use are actually referring to the saving of Israel, the nation. We too often take statements that are intended for the nation of Israel and apply them to individuals.

An example is in Jeremiah 29 when we read that after seventy years are completed with Babylon I will come to you and fulfill my gracious promise to bring you back to this place…" It is a mistake to interpret this as a promise to individuals. It is a promise to the nation.

The fact that the church created the Bible and not vise-versa helps me to answer the question about whether or not I have to take every word of the Bible as literally true or whether social and cultural ideas influence these writings. This is not an issue designed to debate the inerrancy of the scripture. It is an issue that confronts the idea that every word of the Bible must be accepted as literally true because that concept stands in the way of many who would like to believe in God and in Jesus Christ.

A very important point for us to remember is that we are Christians because we believe in the resurrected Christ and not because we believe in an inerrant Bible. This is especially true about the "old" Testament (covenant). Hebrews 8: 13 says that old covenant is obsolete. Thank God, accepting Biblical inerrancy is not necessary for our salvation.

Chapter 9

Must we believe every word in the Bible is literally true?

I love the Bible and read from it every day but I do not worship the Bible. It is a source for me. I learn about acts of God and the truth about Jesus by studying it but I am not a literalist. You may be a literalist and that is certainly alright. But I think we all need to maintain enough humility to admit that we can be wrong. I obviously believe I am right to reject the literalist view of the scriptures.

I closed the previous chapter on the church and scripture by raising this issue.

Theologian Karl Barth wrote that he took the Bible far too seriously to take it literally. L'Engle says, "There is no way that you can read the entire Bible seriously and take every word literally. Contradictions start in the first chapter of Genesis. There are two creation stories, two stories of the making of Adam and Eve. And that is all right. The Bible is still true."

L'Engle, further notes that we read history and think that is where we find out what really happened. She notes that the history of the "Civil" war depends on who is writing it. Her mother was a Southerner and her father a "damn Yankee." They told the story from two different perspectives but they both told the truth.

Some people still debate over the "seven days" of creation as if God created in human time. Scripture does make it clear that God's time and our time are not the same. The old hymn notes that 'a thousand ages in God's sight are but a moment past. So L'Engle says, "Why get so upset about the idea that God might have created in divine time, not human time. What kind of a fact is this that people get so upset about?" Facts are static, even comfortable, even when they are wrong. Truth pushes us to look in new ways that are not comfortable so we often resist it. "Facts" are not necessarily "truth."

"The Bible is not objective. Its stories are passionate, searching for truth (rather than fact) and searching most deeply in story." The story of David is complex and fascinating with its many prefigures of Jesus. L'Engle in working on her book

"Certain Women" said she discovered many more contradictions than she had remembered or expected. There were two different versions of Saul's death and two different ways of bringing David into the story. The biblical writer was simply trying to tell the truth about King David and the truth is more important than details (facts).

Jesus used stories to make points that were true. The stories were not factual (no one had a plank in his eye) but it was true in that we are unwilling to see our own enormous faults and we are eager to point out much smaller faults in other people. In "The Meaning of Truth" there is the note that "literalism is a terrible crippler." Then there is added "I wish the church would be brave enough to acknowledge that there are questions to which, during our mortal lives, we have no answers...And unless we allow truth to be a widening light, we hamstring ourselves. Love, for instance is beyond the realm of provable fact." Still we believe in it and are seeking to understand more.

Stories enable us to find meaning. The stories in the Bible, even those that are not literally true, help us to find and affirm meaning in our lives. That is truth.

Just because something is written in the Bible does not mean that it must be taken as "the Word of God" in all instances. I have heard ministers say about their views, "The Bible says it. I believe it. That settles it." That is a blind stance that ignores the influence of early church leaders to include their ideas and beliefs in the Bible and it ignores inconsistencies and contradictions in the Bible. The Bible tells us about God but it is not God!

Fortunately we can reverence and study the scriptures without being forced to accept them as all to be accepted as literal. There are some clear examples that cannot be meant to be literal and many examples that can at least be questioned.

Our faith in God must not be contingent on our faith in the Bible. What if we lived in the two or three hundred years before there was a Bible? People believed in God during those years. We are fortunate to have the Bible but our faith in God goes far beyond the written words of the Bible.

In fact I am among those who believe that the early framers of the Bible made a serious mistake by including both the Jewish Covenant, (Old Testament) and the new covenant between God and His people (New Testament) in one book. It would have served all of us better if they had designated the "Jewish Bible" and the "Christian Bible" as two separate books. If we begin reading either Matthew or Luke we will get a clearer picture of Jesus than if we begin with Genesis. The Old and the New are different.

It is probably true that the Old is no longer binding, (It is obsolete. Hebrews 8:13), on Christians but the New requires even more of us. Jesus certainly didn't permit the Old laws to get in his way when healing on the Sabbath, eating with tax collectors, and talking with Samaritans. More than the walls came down when the temple was destroyed in 70 AD.

Our belief in a moral code implies the existence of God. We cannot make up our own moral guidelines. Good and evil are determined and defined by God. The only explanation for universal moral guidelines is the existence of a holy God.

I continue to ask questions because my relationship to God and my belief in Him are far too important not to examine. I want to know the truth about God, about faith, about Jesus, about the Bible and related issues. Jesus said we would know the truth and the truth would make us free. We must not be reluctant to look for truth where ever we can find it.

Look at some of those examples.

I Corinthians 11 is a passage (verses 2-16) where Paul goes into detail about why it is wrong for a woman to pray without covering her head and it is wrong for a man to cover his head when praying. Is this the "Word of God" on this practice or does this grow out of social customs of the day and some early stories from the Old Testament?

This does not mean that we are no longer to keep the laws of God verified by Jesus. It does mean that the additional laws included by the early Rabbis are not necessarily mandated for Christians. Examples are circumcision, ceremoniously washing before eating anything, clean and unclean foods.)

An interesting observation is made that the reason for a woman covering her head when she prays grows from the rather strange (and questionable?) story from Genesis 6:1-4. The Genesis passage says that angels seeing the attractiveness of women came down and engaged in sex with them and this is given as a reason for Giants being born. The evidence of this is then alluded to in 1 Corinthians 11: 10. Here Paul says that women should cover their heads when they pray because of the angels. I have difficulty believing that a literal acceptance of these passages is not only not necessary but in error. In fact, they have been used to "keep women" in their place by modern day church men.

In I Corinthians 14: 34-35 Paul says that women are to keep silent in the church. I am sure that he was referring to the meeting of the congregation and not to an organized meeting in a church building. Nevertheless, it would be difficult to miss the strong role of women in the early church. Phoebe was a deaconess. Lois, Timothy's grandmother, Dorcas, and many others are named as leaders are named in the New Testament.

Jesus certainly recognized and appreciated the contributions of women in his ministry. Women were first to see the empty tomb and first to carry the message of the resurrection. That is a tremendous responsibility carried by women in the first days after the resurrection.

I don't want to make light of the problem but I can imagine if a woman asked a question in a church meeting and Paul said, "Be quite and ask your husband at home." A woman might well have answered, "This is my home." It is possible that the meeting was in the home of that woman and her family since the early church often met in homes of the congregation.

Without tongue in cheek I would point out that it could seem ridiculous to take every word literally. How much wine can an elder drink and still serve? How about divorced people serving in the church? Can they not be forgiven and accepted as servants in the church. Some have tried to by-pass the command that they should be husbands of one wife by saying that means one wife at a time.

Why can't we just accept the fact that sometimes literal interpretations get in the way of understanding the greater message which is that we are to act toward one another in love. That is the Command of Jesus. Was Paul writing the inspired truth of God in Galatians 3:28 when he said that in Christ there is no male or female but all are one in Him? If he was writing truth then was he also writing truth when he wrote to the Corinthians that it is a shame for women to speak in church? Do we think that God told him to make the harsh statements about women to accommodate the cultural ideas?

I note that Jesus didn't seem to accommodate cultural ideas in his teaching and in his living. He, in fact, confronted many cultural ideas and ultimately it was this approach that brought about His execution. It is hard for me to believe that God lead Paul to write accommodating cultural ideas. If Paul wrote "the word of God" he surely would have noted that God accepts all people equally.

A simpler possibility is that Paul was wrong and perhaps inclined to be accommodating on the issue of women because it actually was what he thought. I have admiration for Paul as a great Christian teacher and leader but he was not perfect. None of the human beings who wrote the Bible were perfect. There was only one perfect and that was Jesus.

This is an important issue because it affects the way many view women as inferior and not able to be leaders in the church. That is an unfortunate conclusion based on questionable scriptures or at least questionable application of scriptures. This is an important issue for individuals who are directly affected.

It may not seem like much to many but years ago (in the 1960's) in our church we decided to take a clear stand for equality between the sexes. This meant that we would ordain woman to serve in the same offices occupied by men. We ordained women to serve as deacons. That was far more important to some women that we could have imagined.

I received this note from a woman who was ordained as a deacon in our church. She said she wanted us to know that serving as a deacon was and honor and privilege for her. Then she wrote after she was ordained, "The morning after I was ordained I spent the morning alone with God in my kitchen. It was awesome. I cried all morning and I now have the confidence that I can do a good job...please feel free to ask us if there is any way we can help." One woman was encouraged with the action that we took. It was far more important than we realized.

There are well meaning Christians who believe that Paul was simply accommodating himself to the culture of his time. That does not seem to me to be an adequate explanation. I don't want to sound too harsh but I believe that if it is wrong today to not treat women with respect as equals, it was also wrong in Paul's day. What is right is right and what is wrong is wrong.

Look at racial prejudice. Was it wrong in New Testament times or did it just become wrong in modern days? I believe it was always wrong. Jesus did not accommodate himself to culture and accept prejudice when he dealt with the Samaritans. He honored them and treated them with respect, acceptance and love. That is the standard for how we are to treat people of all races and sexes. Our guide is the love of Jesus.

This was all important to Paul because he was instructed to reach the Gentiles and was not to force them to obey the Old Testament laws concerning circumcision and the like. He embraced the Great Commandment, to love God and to love your neighbor and believed, what Jesus taught, that the whole law was summed up in the "golden rule."

The valid question we should be asking as we read the scriptures is "How can we apply this in the spirit of the love of Jesus?" That is the fundamental question for Christians.

Most Atheists reject moral guidelines because they simply do not believe in God. "God teaches us" has no meaning to them. But the fact that we have inclinations to know that there is good and evil in the world, that there is right and wrong, is an argument for the existence of God.

Romans 1: 20 – 32 is a passage where Paul lists things that he apparently believed we all should know were wrong. Look at the list. Everyone should know that being filled with unrighteousness, wickedness, greed, evil, full of envy, murder, strife, deceit, malice, gossiping, slandering, hating God, being insolent, arrogant, inventors of evil, disobedient to parents, without understanding, untrustworthy, unloving, unmerciful; and although they know the ordinance of God, they still practice these things. Paul believed that we should know that all these things are wrong and we are without excuse when we practice them.

Paul contends that we all should know these things because they are "written in our hearts and on our consciences (Romans 2: 15). We don't just come up with the ideas about what is good and what is evil on our own. Those ideas have their origin in God. That is my belief. I don't have to believe that every word of the Bible is literally true. Many of the words are not true and we should be able to accept that. That does not diminish at all our faith in God and our faith in Jesus. I repeat, we are not saved because we believe in an inerrant book but because we believe in Jesus. I believe that the Bible is true but I still have questions.

Chapter 10

Can we Blend the Old and New Testaments?

Testament is just another word for covenant, or agreement. So can we blend the old and new covenants? The short answer is "no." But that doesn't stop us from trying and in the trying we really contaminate our theology in the attempts. We have become use to seeing the "Hebrew Bible" (Old Covenant) and the "Christian Bible" (New Covenant) combined with the same cover and that makes it really difficult for us to separate them. They are different and there is no question but that the "Old Covenant) is no longer binding. Jesus fulfilled it and as Jeremiah predicted long ago, the Old Covenant passes away (Jeremiah 31: 31-32).

I briefly called attention to this earlier but want to be more explicit. If I say that the Old Covenant has passed away and is obsolete there will be objection from people who are clinging to the "old." Let me rather quote from the Bible itself concerning the Old Covenant. The writer of Hebrews says that Jesus brings a more excellent ministry and is the mediator of a "better covenant" (Hebrews 8: 6). The writer then says that God will "Effect a new covenant" (Hebrews 8: 8).

This new covenant will be written upon the hearts of the people (8:10. But note this statement from Hebrews 8: 13. **"When he said, 'A new covenant,' he has made the first obsolete. But whatever is becoming obsolete and growing old is ready to disappear."** Can the message be any clearer than that? The Old Covenant is now obsolete and has disappeared. The old tabernacle is no longer because Christ is a greater and more perfect tabernacle (Hebrews 9:11). He could not do this "while the outer tabernacle was still standing 9: 8)."

We need to let go of the old and embrace the new. The new is better. It is based on the life and death of Jesus. This is a more important issue than a lot of people realize. Christians would be a lot more able to understand the New Testament (New Covenant) if their Bible (Christian Bible) was separated from the Old Covenant (Jewish Bible). We need to find the courage to separate them. That does no disservice to either Bible. It just separates them.

Absolutely great reading that helps clarify this fact is found in Andy Stanley's writing. His book "Irresistible" is tremendously helpful. After making a solid case for the ending of the "Old Covenant" he writes "Resist the temptation to resolve theological, ideological, or ethical conflicts between the Old Testament and "**the teaching of Jesus and the apostles.**"

Even believing this, I have difficulty separating and not trying to somehow rationalize the differences. I know in my mind that the "Old" is no longer applicable as ethical and religious guidelines but I find it hard to accept and apply this truth that I do believe. I want to do it and in order to do that I have to remember that "that was then," and "this is now." Culture was different, faith was different, and revelation" of God was different. When I rationally look at the difference it becomes clear that I need to stop trying to tie the two (Old and New) together. They don't fit and never will.

I do not apply very many of the ideas in the Old Covenant to my life. I do not believe Gentiles have to be circumcised in order to become Christians. I do not believe adulterers should be stoned to death. I do not believe in "an eye for an eye." I do not believe we should destroy those who do not agree with us and a lot of other things that are taught in the Old Covenant (Testament)

I respect the inspiring stories told in the Old Testament and some of the poetry is encouraging but I do not find guidance for my life in them. I read, even study, some of the prophets and how they looked for a Messiah but I remember that their scholars (the Pharisees) totally missed the coming of the Messiah.

My faith in Jesus does not rest on accepting the Old Testament as "the Word of God." It doesn't even rest on accepting the New Testament as the "word of God." My faith in Jesus is grounded in my belief in His death burial and resurrection from the dead. These were doctrines that influenced my life before I ever read the Bible. I was taught these doctrines by my grandmother from the time I was a small child.

I learn from the words of Jesus, recorded in the Bible, from the words of John, Peter, Paul, James, and other apostles recorded in the Bible but I believe them because they are true and not because they are written in the Bible.

I grow weary of the Christian teachers who labor to make apparent contrary teaching somehow fit together. There is no point in that. Relax and let the teaching of Jesus bring comfort and grace into your life. He is the key.

I am sure that this bothers some people but we really need to separate our "faith in Jesus" from what we have believed was the infallible Bible. It is not infallible but Jesus is.

Chapter 11

Did Jesus influence interpretation of scripture?

Another question for me is "How did Jesus influence our interpretation of scripture? Did he add anything, change anything, or teach us deeper meanings? Does He change any of our views or interpretations?" I believe the answer must be "absolutely yes." John chapter 8 gives us a clear example of this, as do several other passages. This passage is referenced in the following list of differences that Jesus made. The Sermon on the Mount moves us from Old Testament ideas of destroying our enemies to loving our enemies.

It is certainly clear that Jesus made some changes in the law. Look at Matthew chapter 5. There are six examples in this one chapter where Jesus is quoted as saying, "You have heard it said.....but I say unto you." See verses Matthew 5: 21-22, 27-28, 31-32, 33-34, 38-39, and 43-42.

1. The first of these examples reveals how Jesus deepened the commandment about murder. He said, "You have heard that it was said to people long ago, 'Do not murder...' But I tell you that anyone who is angry with his brother will be subject to judgment." It is no longer just the physical act of murder that is judged but also the spiritual act of anger. That makes the law deeper and more spiritual in meaning.

2. The second example is in verses 27-28 where Jesus "You have heard that is was said, 'Do not commit adultery.' But I tell you that anyone who looks at a woman lustfully has already committed adultery with her in his heart.'" Again, the command is extended to include thoughts as well as action.

3. In verses 31-32 He deepens the "to have a certificate for divorce" to say that He does not approve of divorce for any cause except unfaithfulness. That made it more difficult to get a divorce.

4. In verses 33-34 He changes "do not break your oath" to make no oath at all. Just let your answers be yes or no anything beyond that is from evil (probably means, just be honest and not without trust.)

5. In verses 38-44 He makes a dramatic change from "eye for eye and tooth for tooth to 'Do not resist an evil person and if someone strikes you on the right cheek, turn to him the other...'"

6. In verses 43-44 He says, "Love your neighbor and hate your enemy" is changed to "Love your enemies and pray for those who persecute you." That is a tremendously big step and demands so much spiritual strength that we will have to have His help in following the command. It should be noted that Jesus personified this command when he prayed for the people who were crucifying Him.

Other examples include John 8, where a woman caught in adultery was brought to him because the law demanded that she be stoned to death. He said, "Let those without sin cast the first stone..." His grace, love, and forgiveness deepened the plain statements of law. Law now was seen as something to be interpreted in the light of grace and love. He did not destroy the law but neither did He extend it. He restated it in terms of Love.

He makes the most difficult teachings to be easier to understand because He removed the negative spirit when it exists.

Are there commands, especially in the Old Testament that we should ignore or reject?? For example Killing pregnant women and slaughtering their babies? I cannot believe such commands actually come from God. I believe those who wrote such things only thought they were from God.

The law says that if a man marries a woman and discovers that she is not a virgin, he is to take her back to her family and they are to stone her to death. (Deuteronomy 22: 21-32). Such laws are obsolete (Hebrews 8:13). Thank God.

Chapter 12

Are there inconsistencies and contradictions in the Bible?

Of course there are. This is a difficult question for those who believe the Bible literally and that every word of it is the inspired word of God. These well meaning people will make every effort to rationalize the inconsistencies. They will do this as an effort to defend Christian faith. The effort is not necessary because our faith is not dependent on the absence of inconsistencies. Still they, along with contradictions, are there. In fact, there are 101 inconsistencies listed in an article on the internet.

My first response to that fact is "so what?" Why is that surprising since the Bible was put together with stories, scrolls, and traditions over a period of thousands of years. It is a wonder that it has held together as well as it has or, I would say, it is miraculous. Unless you believe that God mechanically controlled the writing there would be many inconsistencies. There are.

Andy Stanley speaks to this issue in his book, "Irresistible." He writes, "I recently read a blog by a former worship leader who left the faith after she read a book, 'proving' contradictions in the Bible. Apparently, she grew up believing the foundation of our faith is a non-contradictory book.

It is not."

That is an important observation. There are definitely contradictions and inconsistencies in the Bible. God must have chosen imperfect people to write it and put it together. He had to do that since there has been only one perfect person available and He was busy revealing God through actions in His life.

Perhaps the right question is "are there facts and events being described even though there are inconsistencies?" For the answer to that question is, "yes."

Most of the time, when I have confronted the inconsistencies and contradictions, I have been able to accept them and find facts and events revealed by them. Several examples follow....

In Genesis 1 and 2 we find that man was created after the other animals (verses 24-27) and in chapter 2, verses man was created before the animals. The order is not important to me but the bottom line is. The bottom line is that God created mankind.

There is no denying the inconsistencies but when we look for the fact or faith that is revealed in these early chapters of Genesis we find a consistent faith that God created.

In the New Testament there are three different stories about Peter being chosen as a disciple (Matthew 4:18-20, Luke 5:2-11, John 1: 35-42). For me the fact is that Peter was chosen. That is consistent in all the accounts and how or when is of little consequence.

Hell is described as a furnace of fire (light) Matthew 3:12 and 13-42). In Matthew 8:12 and 22: 13 hell is described as "outer darkness." Is it light, fire, or darkness? The bottom line for me is that it is described as a bad place.

Did the Devil take Jesus to the pinnacle of the temple, then to the mountain top (Matthew 4: 5-8) or did he first take Him to the mountain top, then to the pinnacle of the temple (Luke 4: 5-9). The truth the writers are trying to convey is that Jesus was not tempted to choose the kingdoms of this world over doing what He believed was the Father's will.

Did Judas make his deal with the chief priests before the meal (Mt. 26:14-25, Mk 14: 10-11, Luke 22: 3-23) or after the meal (John 13:21-30)? Probably before but John was writing years later and doesn't seem too concerned about being consistent with times. He was just interested in telling the story.

Did the centurion himself approach Jesus to ask for the healing of his servant (Mt. 8:5-12) or did the centurion send elders to do the asking (Lk. 7:2-10)? I don't know the answer to that but the bottom line for me is that the centurion wanted to have his servant healed and Jesus healed him.

Who was Moses father-in-law (Jethro, Exodus 3:1) or (Hobab, Numbers 10 29 and Judges 4: 11)? I don't know why this discrepancy but unless you are worried that

God didn't control every word of the Bible then what difference does it really make?

There are many more clear examples but maybe one more will suffice to get across the point I'm trying to make. Did Judas hang himself after he betrayed Jesus (Matthew 27: 5)? Or did he fall headlong and burst open as his bowels gushed out (Acts 1: 18)? Probably the point is that Judas felt terrible guilt about his actions. We should recognize that the result of betraying Christ in our lives will also bring great guilt. We all need God's grace to face those feelings and that reality.

Are we responsible for making a choice about believing in Jesus or is it impossible to choose Jesus without being drawn to do so by God? (John 5:38-47 vs. John 6:44) I don't know the answer to that question but I know that I want to choose to follow Jesus. Foreknowledge, choice, responsibility, and freedom are all wrapped up together. Maybe they are all true and exist as parallels until they meet in eternity. I just choose Jesus.

Family reunions have shed some light on inconsistencies for me.

I grow weary of looking for inconsistencies and contradictions. The stories and accounts are good enough for me as they are written. You ought to have heard the stories that were told at my family reunions over the years. There were plenty of inconsistencies but I loved and will cherish those stories for the rest of my life.

One special story from those reunions illustrates my point. I heard this story from at least five different sources over the years. It is the story of how my grandfather, Harvey was going on a date with my grandmother, Lela. He arrived and found another young man knocking on her door and trying to get a date with her.

There was a confrontation and then a fight. The story goes, "It wasn't much of a fight. There were only two licks hit. Harvey hit him and he hit the ground." I heard the story several times with varying details like, who was present, who started the confrontation, was my grandmother present or inside her house, and was it on the front lawn or on the road in front of the house. No matter how the details changed the punch line was always exactly the same, "There were two licks hit. Harvey hit him and he hit the ground."

The story tellers were not trying to lie about details. They just didn't matter. The point was to get to the punch line and it was consistent. I believe Biblical story tellers were usually uninterested in details but wanted to get to the point of their stories.

If the story was about creation, the point was "God created the world." That was consistent. No matter if man or animals were created first, the point was that God created them.

In the New Testament the story about the centurion's slave being healed the story teller didn't care if the centurion came to Jesus personally or sent an elder, he or she just wanted to get to the point. The point was consistent. The servant was seriously ill and Jesus healed him. That never changed. We doubtlessly worry too much about minor details and sometimes even miss the main points.

I do not always remember the details but I know my ancestors were trying to tell me about my grandfather. I do always remember the punch line. "There were two licks hit. Harvey hit him and he hit the ground." I still smile at the memory and I am at peace with the memories, "God created it all." And the memory, "The servant was ill and Jesus healed him."

The point here is to focus on the things that matter. I don't care much about the details of how Peter came to be a disciple but I am comfortable with the memory that he did become a disciple and was a leader in the early church.

Chapter 13

What is the Best Thing we can do with our lives?

The best answer that I have seen to this question was illustrated by Viktor Frankl. He said that a chess master was asked, "What is the best move in a game of chess? "

He answered, "There is no best move. It all depends on the situation and the moves of your opponent." Probably there is not one best thing that we can do with our lives. It will always depend on the situation and what is going on around us.

There certainly are a lot of good things we can do with our lives each day. I saw a man in a nursing home recently. He was having trouble moving around in a heavy walker. It was difficult to help him move. His balance was not good and the walker was heavy and bulky. It seemed to me that he needed help so I tried to help him.

It took about thirty minutes and I was exhausted when I left. I was never able to get him to where ever it was that he wanted to go. I had to leave him standing in his room but he didn't seem to be bothered. I left wondering what I could have done to help him. The answer was that there was nothing more I could do then.

I left not feeling good about not being able to help him. What was the best thing I could have done with that thirty minutes? I like to think it was about all I could have done under the circumstances. There are events like that often in our lives. There is no one best thing we can do. It all depends on the situation.

Another important thing to remember when trying to answer the question about the best thing we can do with our lives is that we may not be able to do any really dramatic thing or anything that will cover a long time. What we can do is make the most of the small opportunities that we have.

Call someone who lives alone and see if there is anything they need. Let them know you are thinking about them and be prepared if they have a favor to ask to do your best to help.

Visit seriously ill people that you know. Again, check with them in advance to see if the time is good for them and if it is, visit with them. I have never regretted making such visits.

Still I search for the things that may be best for me to do. I don't always do them, even when they are apparent but I continue to make attempts. That is what we can do.

Some days the best thing we can do is simply go to work or visit with friends. Do whatever you find to do and fulfill the moment.

Chapter 14

Can we Find Answers to all the mysteries in the Bible?

The answer is no but that does not mean we should stop seeking to understand more.

Years ago I was taught ("tongue In cheek") that if someone asked me a question that was too difficult to answer, I should just throw up my hands and say, "Behold, a mystery." I have had many opportunities to follow that advice. There may be some mysteries that I will never understand but I will continue to seek answers.

The existence of a Holy Trinity is a mystery. How can three persons make up God? I don't know. I have heard a lot of solutions in my sixty plus years as a Christian minister but none really cleared up the "mystery."

Examples: I have been told that the three are really just three different functions of God and they are called three different names. When I ask, "Why" I have been told that was just the way God wanted to do it. God certainly can do things any way that He chooses but that still leaves me wondering.

I have been told that the 'three persons in the trinity are like water, ice, and steam. They are different but still the same. I still see it as a mystery. Father, Son, and Holy Spirit are not like water, ice and steam to me. I just don't know. Maybe it is that we just call them by different names but it seems that the New Testament reveals them as "three in one." But I am still looking for the word "trinity" in the New Testament.

Though this is not a satisfactory answer, it is true to the history of the doctrine. The 7th verse of 1 John 5: 7 (KJV) says "There are three that bear record in Heaven, the Father, the Word, and the Holy Ghost, and these three are one." Most Christian commentaries are in agreement that this was not a part of any of the Greek versions of 1 John until Erasmus added it after 1500 AD long after John's death.

A more accurate translation of 1 John 5: 6-7 is "And it is the Spirit who bears witness, because the Spirit is truth. For there are three that bear witness, the spirit and the water and the blood: and the three are in agreement."

The rather simplistic explanation given to me by some who were in seminary with me still seems inadequate. As indicated above they said it is like water, steam, and ice. All are water but different forms. I never found that a very satisfactory analogy. I have not found a definite answer.

The fact that we cannot explain it does not rule out the idea of a trinity but it does not make the claim valid either. I personally believe God, the Father, God, the Son, and God, the Holy Spirit is a fair statement of faith in God as expressed in all three. That doesn't explain the trinity but it is close enough for me.

Chapter 15

A question of greater mystery is in the person of Jesus Christ. How can He be fully God and fully man?

This is where I throw up my hands and say, "Behold a mystery." Honestly I believe that somehow Jesus is fully God and fully man but don't ask me how to explain that.

One of my professors tried to explain this by saying this is a truth that is like "parallel lines" that come together. He said that in theory parallel lines come together in Eternity (somewhere out there). He said that he believed that the truth about Jesus being fully God and fully man will come together in Eternity. I can't argue with that. It just pushes the mystery a step further back. Anyway the Savior has to be fully God and fully human.

The closest thing to a full statement of this idea is in Philippians 2: 5 – 11. This passage says that Jesus emptied Himself and became a man. He lived among us and humbly died on the cross. He was then lifted up so that every knee should bow to Him forever.

One scripture passage that gives an example of growth toward understanding more about Jesus being both God and man is in John chapter 9. In this chapter Jesus heals a blind man and the blind man is questioned by the authorities who are trying to discredit Jesus. It is an interesting story and adds some clarity to at least the healed man's understanding.

The blind man is asked who healed him and he said it was "the man" Jesus. He said that he knew nothing about Jesus except that he made him able to see. He surely thought of Jesus as a wonderful man. Barclay says "we do well sometime to think of the sheer magnificence of the manhood of Jesus." He says further that in any gallery of the world's heroes Jesus must find a place. He is surely one of the loveliest men who ever lived." "Whatever else is in doubt, there is never any doubt that Jesus was a man among men."

The blind man, now seeing, calls Jesus a prophet. He believed that anyone who brought God's message to men, as in healing, is more that the average man. He is a prophet of God.

The man was then found by Jesus in the Temple and Jesus asked him if he believed in the "Son of God." The man said who is he? Jesus said I who am speaking to you is He." The man already believing in the greatness of Jesus now adds, "I believe" and he worshiped Jesus. If we have experienced any love from Jesus or experience any of His grace in our lives we are surely ready to accept Him as more than a mere man. He is the Son of God or fully God. I have continued to search for answers.

Here are conclusions from my research. This is an essential doctrine to Christianity. Christians believe that Jesus is both fully God (described in the New Testament as having all the attributes of God). He is also described as man, a sinless man.

He was born of a woman (human) and fathered by God's spirit (Divine). This is what is taught in the New Testament as an explanation as to how He could be both man and God. He was so fully man that he was persecuted and executed. He died. That is a human characteristic. He was also so fully God that he arose from the dead. Being raised to life is a divine characteristic. Accepting by faith that these things as true we conclude that Jesus was fully human and fully divine.

I have found this faith to be stated and affirmed but I have not found an explanation for it. I cannot prove this but I accept it as true. There will probably always be some ideas about God, salvation, and faith that we will not be able to understand. Still we can ask, but stop before we go crazy!

When I think of Him being a man I add "but a lot more than a man." He was human but he was extraordinary from any of our standards. His influence is so great that it seems more than human.

Here are some things that indicate his power and influence. His birth is the pivotal point of human history. There was history before him but that was changed with His birth. He and his disciples have changed the history of the world. His teachings and example have influenced millions of people to become more than they ever could have been without Him. Our calendars reflect the impact of Jesus birth.

A man but more than a man, he was a man who touched people and made them well. A man who ate fish, got thirsty and requested water from a Samaritan woman and a man who got tired like other men do. He fell asleep in the rear of a boat during bad weather. He was a man who became lonely and requested that His disciples join him in prayer and especially his prayer in Gethsemane.

When we focus on Him we can become less self-centered. Life is not all about me. It is about God and God's love for all of us. We can become less greedy and lustful. We become new people.

A man, yes but he was also God. He said of Himself that He was one with the father. He said that if anyone saw Him they had seen the father. He calmed a stormy sea with words ("Peace, be still.") That is a God action. He fed a multitude with little food, either by example or by a miracle of increase. That is a God action. Then He capped it off by being raised from the dead. He was and is fully man and fully God. That is my faith.

The record in the New Testament clearly characterizes Him as a man. Then He is shown to be more than a man by all the things He did. We may not be able to understand how this can be but our faith says it must be if He is our Savior.

Chapter 16

Does prayer make a difference?

The question is does God answer prayer. Maybe we need to understand more about prayer before we answer that question. We will understand more if we know what the purpose of prayer is. It is not a way to change God. The purpose of prayer is not to convince God to do things differently for us. It is to prepare us to do things for God. This is why it is important to spend a lot of time in prayer. Jesus said that if we abide in him and His word abides in us we can ask what we will and it will be done. (John 15:7)

The primary purpose of prayer is to bring our lives into conformity to God's will for us. Prayer is not to change God but to change us. That does not mean that we will not see answers to our prayers but it does mean that in all probability the answers come to us when we are prepared to receive them.

My youngest daughter was critically ill when she was a baby. I stood outside the window to her hospital room and prayed for her life to be spared. She was convulsing and crying. I was crying, too. As I stood there praying for her life to be spared, I was overcome with the knowledge that no matter what happened, I could trust in God's love.

It was with that awareness that I prayed, "God, I want her to live but if that is not your will I want your will to be done." Still praying, I left the hall and went to the waiting room. In a couple of hours, the doctor came in and told us that our daughter would be all right. Breathing relief, I just thanked God for His love and grace and went back to view my little girl, lying quietly in her bed.

I do not believe that my prayer changed God's will for her. She probably would have recovered anyway. What my prayer did was to change my outlook, no matter what happened. The prayer changed me.

Why are some prayers answered while others are not? I don't know the answer to that unless the purpose of the prayer was all along to change us. If we are not willing to be changed, that prayer cannot be answered. That doesn't mean that we will not see other results. It just means that the primary purpose must not be to get something from God but to bring our lives into conformity with His will.

Prayer is a request for help. That help may come in a lot of forms. It is a matter of faith to look for the answers in whatever happens. That prayer certainly can be accompanied with thanksgiving. Giving thanks makes us more receptive to God's grace.

When we understand the primary purpose of prayer it becomes something more than praying for results in things and others. It is not just asking for things. It is talking to God and listening for God. Prayer is communicating with God and listening for Him to communicate with us.

It is also helpful to know that prayer involves doing as well as saying. We can pray that God will help us do the right things but unless we actively seek the right things to do He cannot help us.

We have records of people who testify that many prayers were answered...as in Mueller, the great English minister who pioneered in serving children, praying for help in meeting the needs of children in England. His prayers were not for himself but for others. In other words, he was praying unselfishly. I would guess that he had prayed for God to bring him into harmony with His will before He prayed for the needs of the children.

My own experience with prayer is that sometimes I have seen what seemed to be miraculous results of healing and other times no healing occurred. Looking back I think that the visible results had nothing to do with whether or not the prayers were being answered.

For many years I spent long periods of time every day praying. I incorporated readings and writing in those times. I confess that I was not responding well to God in my own life and the prayers did not help me to bring my life into harmony with God. In fact, I could leave prayer times with selfish thoughts and sinful desires in my mind. The inconsistency of that did not occur to me for years.

I look back now and know that the prayers were consistent with what I should have been doing. I just didn't follow through. That is probably a result of lack of understanding and certainly lack of discipline on my part.

I am writing this from the perspective of one who believes in God and one who expected to find concrete answers to my prayers. My focus in looking for those concrete answers no doubt kept me from seeing the potential of God working in my life. For me the prayer that meant the most, when prayed honestly, was "God let your will be done."

Praying certainly makes a difference, if not in healing and helping others, always, if understood, makes a difference in me. After all, the primary purpose of prayer is to bring our lives into harmony with Jesus.

Chapter 17

What about Heaven?

Where will it be? What will we do there? Will we recognize and remember people who are there? Will we remember things we did?

We talk about wanting to go to Heaven when we die. We have some vague ideas about what that might be like and a few definite thoughts as to what we hope it will be but there is no way we can know what the reality of it is or may be.

We know from the New Testament that it will not be on earth because we read that this earth will be destroyed (2Peter 3: 7 and following). Revelation 21 probably gives us the most information we have about what it may be like. It will be a new heaven and earth because the first heaven and earth will have passed away.

What we believe is that heaven is where God is and where Jesus is at His right hand and most people would say, "That's good enough for me." But Revelation goes further. It says that God will be with us and be our God and we will be His people.

It further says, and this is our hope and faith, that there will be no more pain, no more grief, and no more death for the former things will all pass away. The promise here is that "God, Himself, will wipe away the tears from" our eyes.

It is doubtful that this will be a place where angels are playing harps and sitting on clouds. We simply do not know what it will be like in detail but most of us hope we will be there.

I believe we will know people there but that presents a problem. Would we then know people who were not there? This is another area of mystery for me. We have testimonies from people who have "died" and come back. Some tell of seeing relatives and wishing to stay with them and not come back to life.

Roy, a great friend of mine, was critically ill at a time when I was about to leave town. I stopped by the hospital to visit him. He had been bed fast with a serious blood disorder, I was surprised when I arrived at the hospital to find him standing in the bathroom, shaving. I said, "Wow, you sure have improved."

He laughed and said, "Jesus came to see me last night and healed me. I woke up this morning feeling fine." (This was not an imagined experience. He assured me that he really saw and talked with Jesus.)

We were both encouraged and I told him I was going to be gone for a few days visiting with my grandmother and family a couple of hundred miles away. He wished me a safe journey and assured me he was fine. When I arrived four and a half hours later at my grandmother's home, there was a call waiting for me. My friend had died shortly after I left. I returned and did his funeral.

That experience said to me that it was possible that my friend, Roy, was so close to God in his life that Jesus really appeared to him from the "other side." His appearance removed all concern Roy might have had about dying. It was an experience that has continued to be a source of hope for me.

Experiences like Roy's and those of others who have "died" and come back give us some idea or hope for what may happen after death. Maybe we will see friends and family. One friend, as he was dying, said that he saw his dad waiting at "the gate." Maybe we'll see Jesus. I just don't know.

After listing the names of several saints who had died, the author of Hebrews follows the list with opening lines in the chapter 12 of Hebrews and says in essence, "Since we are surrounded with this great cloud of witnesses, let us run with patience the race that is set before us."

The clear admonition here is that knowing we are being watched by witnesses who have preceded us in death, we should be encouraged to be stronger and better people. If the dead really can observe us as the author of Hebrews asserts, then we have every reason to believe that we will be able to recognize one another in Heaven.

So what will Heaven be like and what will we do there? If Paul is right in 1 Corinthians 2: 9 and following, "No eye has seen, no ear has heard, no mind has conceived, what God has prepared for those who love Him but God has revealed it to us by his Spirit. The Spirit searches the deep things of God..."

If heaven is like described in Revelation 21 and 1 Corinthians 2, I suspect that we will spend a great deal of our "time" praising God and rejoicing that we can be with Him forever. I can only speculate and guess. What I know is that I really want to be in Heaven with God forever!

One problem for people who believe the Old Testament is "the Word of God" is that there is actually no teaching about life after death in the Old Testament. Some people try to find it in passages that have been misinterpreted. One such example is 2 Samuel 12: 23. This passage is often used to give comfort to people who have lost a child.

When reading this passage we need to remember that in the Old Testament the word "Sheol" is used to identify, not the place, but the state of the dead. People who die are believed to be in Sheol. The dead do not return from there.

When David said about his deceased child "I can't bring him back again but someday I will go where he is" he was saying he is dead and cannot be brought back but some day I will die, also.

In commenting on the use of this passage as hope for bereaved parents, Andy Stanley said, "Would I correct a grieving parent's misapplication of this text? Of course not! But I sure as Sheol wouldn't use it at the funeral service either."

The reason Christians can offer hope for reunion with the deceased has nothing to do with the Old Testament but it is a faith that rests on "the empty tomb" of Jesus. Reading the 2 Samuel passage in the light of the New Covenant meaning is viewing it inappropriately.

It is no reflection on the Old Covenant to recognize it for what it is. But we make a mistake when we read New Covenant meanings into Old Covenant promises. The New Covenant is better because it is based on Jesus, who is greater than Moses and greater than the law and the prophets.

Heaven in the Old Testament is not seen as the eternal dwelling place of redeemed people or the people of God. It is where God lives...among the stars...it is up there and we are down here. I am down here but I believe in Heaven as the eternal abode of the people of God.

I believe in Heaven and that belief removes a lot of fear and concern about death. That faith also brings comfort to me when I think of great friends and family members who have preceded me in dying.

Chapter 18

What is Right and Wrong Behavior?

This question can be asked in several different ways. Examples would be "what is good and what is bad" and "what is sinful and what is righteous?" Before we can answer we will need to agree on a standard for what is right and what is wrong. I have recently learned that we usually answer these questions as they are answered in the Old Covenant way based on how they relate to the nation of Israel. We interpret them as to how they relate to us as individuals, not the intended meaning.

Andy Stanley identifies these answers on Old Covenant morality as "vertical answers." In other words they relate to how we respond to God and what that does for us. It is morality with benefits. In terms of the nation Israel it was "if you do what God wants, then He will take care of you." Those consequences promised to the nation are inappropriately applied to individuals.

We learn the same vertical answers from our parents. The idea is that we are to do what is right because it benefits us and not just because it is right. "If you don't do what I tell you, you will get into trouble." Of "I'll tell you what is right and wrong for you to do." I grew up with those answers. I naturally just moved the answers into my relationship with God. I now believe that was a serious mistake.

What is right, in the horizontal interpretation of right and wrong, is what the love of Jesus leads us to do. In that understanding we are not trying to get something from Jesus for being good, we are trying to respond to His love because of what He has already done for us.

If we accept the life and teachings of Jesus as the standard for what is right and wrong we will have a clear set of standards that do not rely on the "law" of the Old Covenant but on the deeper and more challenging standards of the "New Covenant" and the greatest law of loving God and loving our neighbors. As I respond I will be referring to the "Jesus standard."

Looking back on my life I see that all most of my responses in trying to do right were in order to get right standing with God. This would benefit me. It had little to do with what I believed the love of Jesus would lead me to do.

When I committed sin it was because it was something that felt good to me or gave me something that I wanted. I would then ask for forgiveness in order to get more good things or standing from God. Not much, good or bad, was done out of seeking to relate to others on the basis of the love of Jesus.

It is disappointing to me to look back on my life and realize how much of my relationship to God was based on the vertical (Old Covenant) guidelines and very little was based on the horizontal (New Covenant) guidelines of Jesus loving others. I am really trying to live with awareness of the importance of the horizontal relationships. I want my life to impact the world around me and others in my life in a manner that is consistent with the standard set by Jesus.

We are all familiar with the previously mentioned vertical guidelines. The Old Covenant law gave us a lot of guidelines. Most all of them were vertical impacting what we get from our relationship with God.

Even in the Ten Commandments we see this. Honor your father and mother, why? Do this In order that your lives will be longer. It is all about what's in it for me. Jesus brought new meanings in the law. Because of Him, the church began, not celebrating the Sabbath on Saturday but on Sunday. Why? They did it because it was the day of resurrection for Jesus.

When Jesus taught about law, He said the greatest law was to love God with all our hearts, minds, and soul and to love our neighbor as we love ourselves.

When it comes to obeying the commandments of God, read 1Corinthians 13. Paul says that if we do it all right, even to the point of giving our lives as martyrs it benefits nothing unless it is done with love. The clear implication is that we are to do right, not in order to get something, but because we have learned to love and to act out of love for God and for others.

This all becomes clearer when we realize that we think of most of our behaviors as to how they affect God and then as a result what that does for us. If we could learn to base our behaviors on what good they do for others and how they will show the love of God to them our whole perspective changes. We will not want to behave in ways sexually that do not show respect for one another. We will want to treat people as equals and fairly because we want to let the love of God be our guide.

From what Jesus taught and how He lived we should conclude that God is not interested in our burnt offerings or religious rituals, even circumcision. He is interested in how we treat one another. We are instructed to not even make an offering to God if we have ill will or a bad relationship with another person. We are to leave our gift at the Altar and go make it right with our neighbor (Matthew 5:23-24). What a difference the standard of love makes.

The Old Covenant was based on an "I will if you will" guideline. The New Covenant is based on "I have loved you now love one another." That difference is becoming more meaningful and clearer to me as a think about it.

For me the question boils down to what is right and what is wrong when measured by the standards set forth by Jesus. The following are some examples:

When thinking about the question of what is right and what is wrong I am reminded of the time I lived through from the mid 1960s and the early 2000s. The Christians were struggling with some very heavy questions about right and wrong.

There was, of course, the question of race relations. I remember trying to resolve that conflict in the church where I was pastor. It was not hard to know what was right from the words of Jesus. There is absolutely no room for racial prejudice in His teaching.

I preached a position sermon on race relations after I read of the bombing in a Birmingham church that killed three teen aged girls. I announced that we could no long be silent about the prejudice that resulted in that tragedy.

We began looking for ways to confront that problem. It was not always a popular stand to take. One of our members told me that if I didn't stop preaching about the equality of the races there were several members with him who would leave our congregation.

I don't know where I found the words but they came out, "Well if you leave the church because you oppose equality of the races you will do nothing to reduce the quality of spirituality in the church. " For whatever reason, he did not leave the church at that point.

Within a year of that confrontation our congregation voted to join a black church convention. We were subsequently "kicked" out of the Missouri Baptist Convention. We were however able to form some strong relationships with members of the convention we had joined. The point in sharing this story is to point out the difficulty that sometimes follows us when we try to do what we really believe is right.

It is worth the effort!

There were several other issues that challenged us during that time period. There was equal treatment of, not only the races, but the sexes as well. Church people during that period had to make a lot of hard decisions about what seemed right or wrong to them.

Our church made sure that we had an equal number of men and women serving in key positions and that they were all ordained. In other words, we tried to assure that men and women were treated as equals.

Is it right to forgive and try to restore drug addicts and alcoholics? The answer from Jesus would be "Yes." We treated alcoholism as a disease and tried to help the sick recover and reclaim their lives. We believed that this was right and that by seeking to redeem those lives we were acting in unselfish ways...a horizontal standard.

Should divorced people be permitted to serve in churches, as deacons or pastors? The answer from the standpoint of Jesus' forgiveness is yes. Forgiveness has as its purpose to restore and redeem people who have sinned and fallen short of what is right.

At its simplest level, doing right means not doing what we know or believe to be wrong. But doing right is a lot more than just avoiding wrong. It involves consciously and deliberately choosing to right and good things with our lives. This requires discipline and commitment.

There are some things that just seem to be right. It seems to be right to forgive and restore broken lives. If we cannot do that then what are we doing that is different from the world outside our faith? We are to hold ourselves to a higher standard than that the people who do not claim faith in Jesus.

Chapter 19

What is sin?

The Apostle Paul tells us in Romans 3:23 that all of us have sinned. John tells us in 1 John that if any one says he has no sin, he is a liar. Since all of us are sinners we probably ought to be pretty clear on what sin is. Paul says again in Romans that the wages of sin is death. So what is it?

The Greek word for sin in the New Testament is "hamartia" and literally means missing the mark and thus being disqualified from the prize. I am pretty sure the "mark" is doing what is right and the prize is life with God. To miss the mark is pretty serious.

I believe that sin is characterized by weakness and, especially selfishness. Living for ourselves and doing what feels good to us (to me) is an expression of sinning. Selfishness contaminates everything that we do.

Selfishness excludes concern for how our behaviors and attitudes will affect others. Sexual sin is an example of that. If it feels good to us we have very little concern for how it affects anyone else. This is a primary characteristic of sin but there are several other ways to express the meaning of it.

Sin means disobeying guidelines that we know are good. It means doing what we know or at least believe is wrong. It means with holding material things that we could use to meet the needs of others. Again, that is descriptive of "selfishness."

Some specific examples of sin would be lying, stealing, coveting, lusting, being jealous of others, and envying them. Still all of these things can be described as selfish behaviors. Pride (arrogance) certainly falls into the category of selfish attitudes.

It is not always obvious to us but pride really does precede destruction (Proverbs 16:18). A good friend and co-worker and I were talking about prayer and confession of sin when he said, "I know confession of sin is important but I can't think of any sin in my life right now." He was serious and not trying to be funny.

I said to him, "When we can't think of sin in our lives we can begin by making some guesses. One good place to start is 'spiritual pride.'" He grinned and nodded. It is easy to miss but a sin, nevertheless.

Sin is also failure to do good things. It is failing to forgive people when we are offended by them. Sin is waste, waste of time, energy, and resources.

Sin can hurt people physically and/or emotionally. The results of sin are guilty feelings, loss of energy, loss of passion for life. It can, and often does result in a sense of failure and depression. Obviously from all this we can see that it is to be avoided in our lives.

Another important definition of sin is "failure to act in love toward others." After all Jesus taught that the greatest commandment is to love God with all our hearts, minds, and souls and the second is to love our neighbors as we love ourselves (Matthew 22: 37-40).

The love of God, expressed in Jesus Christ is to be our guideline for living. Do you want to avoid sin and do what is right? Then live according to the love of Jesus Christ. To see the tremendous value of living from the heart of love read I Corinthians 13. In this passage Paul tells us that even the good things we do are of no value unless they come from love.

A wonderful guide for avoiding sin and living for what is right can be found in the book "The Anatomy of Peace." The authors of this book recommend that we search our hearts for our best urges and live according to them.

They tell a story about a young Jewish man whose father had been killed by an Arab soldier. He saw an elderly Arabic man begging on the street and felt an urge to help him. Then on second thought he remembered that it was an Arab who killed his father. He walked away. Later he said that he wished he had helped the man...that was the best desire of his heart. When we fail to follow our heart's best desires, we sin.

When we learn to act from our hearts best urges we will be living a life of love. That brings us into obedience to the great commandment as found in Matthew

22. This is where Jesus explains that the greatest commandments are to love God with all our hearts and to love our neighbors as we love ourselves. This brings a sense of peace within us and in our relationships.

The truth about sin is that it hurts everyone it touches. My sin affects my attitudes and my relationships with everyone in my life. It destroys my internal peace and leads to war within and with others on the outside of my life. It is more destructive than we realize.

So in conclusion note that sin involves not only what we do but also what we think about for every thought is to be brought into harmony with Christ. (2 Corinthians 10: 5). When we focus our thoughts on selfish things and think about wrong things we like to do, we are sinning. No wonder Paul told us that we all have sinned and come short of God's glory.

Chapter 20

A Question about Death

How are we to deal with the reality of death?

My brother was recently diagnosed with cancer of the pancreas. That is a serious diagnosis. It can be a fatal condition. I have been concerned about him and have been really interested in how he has dealt with the diagnosis. He had not yet had surgery for the condition and patiently waited for word as to when that would take place. It never did.

I was impressed with the calmness with which he has received the news about his condition. I asked him how he is dealing with the situation. He said "I can't do anything about the fact that I am going to die, if not from this, from something else. I just accept that as a fact and try to do the best I can with the time I have now." That is a wonderful reaction and attitude. I have no way of knowing what the outcome will be in the near future but the situation has set me to thinking about how we can deal with the reality of death.

In a short time he died but he seemed to die with a peace about the process. I believe his attitude made dying less painful for him and for those of us around him.

Death is a reality. I asked my dad one time if he worried about dying. He, in his characteristically light heart ed, manner said, "Why, Bill, there is no reason to worry about dying." Then he stuck out his hand, palm down, and moved it closer to the floor until it was only about knee high. He then said, "Ever since we were about this high we have known we were going to die. There is no reason to worry about it. It will just happen someday."

There was a lot of wisdom in his response. One reaction to the fact of death is to simply accept it as fact. None of us can change that. But once we accept the fact we can begin to act as if it is going to happen and make whatever preparations we need to make and then get on with living "the best we can with the time we have now."

A very good book by Karen Wyatt is "What Really Matters (7 Lessons for Living from the Stories of the Dying.)" A very good chapter in this book is titled "Impermanence." We will live with more peace and be less anxious about death when we realize that every thing is impermanent. Nothing in this world lasts forever, not relationships, not achievements, not material things, riches, or anything else. I am learning to call that reality to my attention many times a day. It helps me to focus on this moment as the only real moment of life that I have. I must live to the fullest the moments I have and recognize that everything is impermanent. That includes all that I see and Me!

Several months ago my brother began making financial arrangements for his wife. He said he didn't want to leave her without making sure she would be taken care of financially. They had already made plans for what they wanted done with their bodies. They have made arrangements to donate their bodies to science.

One thing that all of us can do is decide what we want done with our remains once we die. My wife and I have decided on a funeral home and a cemetery lot. We both want to be cremated and have our ashes buried in one lot.

That is minimal preparation we can all do to deal with the reality of death. We can, as my brother has, make sure we have taken care of financial arrangements so that neither of us nor our surviving family will be without money to meet the needs to carry out our requests and dispose of our worldly possessions.

On a more personal level we can deal with the reality mentally and emotionally. My personal belief is that one of the most important things we can do is to commit ourselves to making the best use of our time now. Senseless worry about dying only diminishes the life we have now.

After a knee replacement and while experiencing the pain of treatment and recovery, I said to my physical therapist, "This experience has caused me to think of the fact that my life is very short and I don't know how long I have to live."

He said to me, "You have the same life expectancy that you have always had. You have today and no assurance of anything more." He was right and that focus helped me to stop most of my worry about the brevity of life and the "not knowing" that I was experiencing. Accept the reality, make all the arrangements that are practical, and focus on making the most of what we have today.

Part of our preparation includes examining our own faith or beliefs about the future. Jesus said that we are not to let our hearts be troubled about the future. He said that we are simply to believe in Him. (John 14)

In the chapter on heaven I have suggested several thoughts about life after death and the promises we from Jesus and other believers concerning that life. Revelation 21 contains the following powerful list of promises from the apostle John. He says that in that after life there will be no longer any pain, no tears, no death because all the former things will have passed away and God will be with us to comfort us and wipe away all tears from our eyes. Those promises can help in dealing with the reality of death.

It would be beneficial to discuss death with family members. That has been helpful for those who have had the wisdom and courage to do it. Here is a simple list of things that can help you and your loved ones to prepare for death.

1. Discuss the feelings you have and that your family has about the fact of dying. It should be a matter of fact discussion and not forced on young family members but not held away from them either. Offer them the opportunity and make it clear that this is an acceptable topic for conversation. A key for talking with children is to give them as much information as they want and not more than they want.

2. Discuss the desires you have and that any of the family members have. Make a written list of those desires and include things like funeral arrangements, casket, clothes for burial, what cemetery you want to use, type of service, preference for people who will be involved in the service, scriptures (if any), and music.

3. List names of insurance companies and location of policies, checking accounts, savings accounts, IRAs, stocks, mortgages, and property titles, and wills if any. Certainly include a "living will" for yourself.

4. Take advantage of discussing this topic to clarify values and priorities.

It is wise to deal with this vital issue at a time when things are calm and sane. Too many people live with the delusion of immortality. While death is inevitable otherwise rational people seem to act as if "it won't happen to me." It will!!

The best advice any of us can receive is to simply accept the facts and prepare in the most practical and realistic ways that we can. I still remember my Boy Scout motto, "Be prepared."

Chapter 21

Other questions we continue to ask

1. What about the environment? Is there anything I can do to protect our environment? I can begin to take care to recycle the paper we are discarding. We are doing that. It isn't much but it is something. I want to do something positive and that is one small thing I can do but I still have questions about what else I can do.

2. What about war and peace?

3. What about over population?

4. What about homelessness and poverty?

5. What about immigration?

I have a lot more questions than answers but I am looking. Following are examples of some attempts to answer some of these question.

It has become popular to speak out against the problems listed above but precious little is being done about them. This is not meant to be a criticism of the people who are sincerely concerned about these issues but it is meant to be realistic. What can we do about these enormous problems?

It seems trite but I believe it is true that our only hope is in beginning to deal with the problems one by one and a little bit at a time. For instance the church I served as senior pastor for more than 51 years tried to deal with the issues in the only ways we knew how.

There are thousands of homeless people in the metropolitan St. Louis area. We cannot solve the problems created for and by these people but we can help some of them. This one church decided to help the homeless by providing sleeping bags for them. A group of people from the church began sewing sleeping bags and distributing them to homeless people who went to missions for help, especially in winter months.

We were able to make more than 500 sleeping bags available and added to that several thousand pairs of socks by collecting them on what we called "Sock it to Me Sundays." We added winter caps. All these were distributed to homeless shelters and inner city missions.

This effort was continued until our church was closed. By that time we had helped several thousand people fight the coldness of winter by wrapping themselves in sleeping bags and wearing socks and winter caps. That was what one church could and did do. Imagine the impact if several hundred churches made the same efforts.

Of course we cannot clean up the country of the messes created by thousands of poor immigrants and homeless people. A recent study concluded that more than 20 million un-skilled jobs will disappear in the next 25 years and be replaced by automation. What will happen to the people who occupy the jobs lost to automation? Many of those workers are immigrants and they are not going to go home. They will still be here and few if any will be trained for other jobs. Most will be angry and wondering what happened to the American dream that they had expected. I don't know the answer but that is a problem.

What we can do is pick up the trash that is around us and do our best to not add to the problem.

The friend in Arizona, I mentioned previously still goes for a walk every morning. Several years ago he began the practice of picking up trash as he took his walk. He picked has up trash every morning for at least the past 15 years. He can't clean up the entire city where he lives but he can help. Huge problems like those we face can only be solved by the efforts of one person, one group, one organization at a time.

Remember the crying Indian? This was an ad that ran repeatedly in the 1970's. I cannot get the image out of my mind. It began with an American Indian man in buckskins paddling a canoe down a stream lined with trees. It is a peaceful scene until a piece of trash floats past the bow of his canoe. It is shocking and becomes repulsive.

The man pulls his canoe onto the shore and behind him is an enormous power plant with smoke pouring from it into the sky. The Indian begins to walk along the shore which is covered with beer bottles and food wrappers. He moves up to a highway and stands as cars roar by.

A man in a white car comes speeding by and throws a paper sack of half eaten fast food out his window. The sack lands on the Indians moccasins and the contents cover his feet. The camera pulls back from the Indian and shows a single tear rolling slowly down his cheek.

The narrator for says, "People start pollution and people can stop it." The solution is to stop throwing trash on our streets and in our rivers and begin to pick up the trash that we see.

Obviously we cannot deal with all the questions we have about life and religion but this is a beginning. Other questions that come to my mind are questions about taking care of the environment, the growing population crisis of this planet, and the wars that continue around the world. It is over whelming to think of all the issues that confront us.

Think of the homeless people sleeping on skid row. There are nearly 2000 sleeping in an area that has nine toilets. That is just the beginning of the problem. I have read that storm drains are clogged with human waste and hypodermic needles are lying on the sidewalks on almost every block. You can read the shocking statistics in the book "Ship of Fools."

I am still looking for answers and will probably do that for as long as I live. I want to find out more about taking care of climate control, war and peace and the over populating of the world. These issues may not impact my life in the short time I have remaining on earth but they will impact my children and their children. That is reason enough for me to keep on searching.

Chapter 22

The Most Important Question for me

What about the Resurrection of Jesus?

While many of the questions asked in this material have to do with Christian concepts this question is clearly strictly a Christian question. The answer is vital, I mean absolutely vital to Christianity. Without the resurrection of Jesus, there can be no Christian faith.

The pastor of the church I frequently attend, Trey Herweck, preached an Easter sermon that really caught my attention. He outlined his thoughts in three sections. I am trying to remember them as accurately as I can. His first point was the question: "What if there was no resurrection of Jesus?" The second question was, "What is the evidence for the resurrection of Jesus? The answer to this question centers on evidence in the New Testament but is not limited to this evidence. The final question is, "What results from the resurrection of Jesus?"

The answer to the first question cannot be over emphasized. The answer is grounded in the writing of Paul in 1 Corinthians 15: 12-19. In this passage Paul notes that some people say there is no resurrection of the dead. He then says, "If there is no resurrection of the dead, then not even Christ has been raised. And if Christ has not been raised our preaching is useless and so is your faith. More than that, we are then found to be false witnesses about God, for we have testified about God that he raised Christ from the dead (verses 13 – 15)."

The impact of this statement from 1 Corinthians can be devastating to Christian faith. Look at the conclusion it in verses 16 – 19). "For if the dead are not raised, then Christ has not been raised either. And if Christ has not been raised, your faith is futile; you are still in your sins. Then whose also who have fallen asleep in Christ are lost. If only for this life we have hope in Christ, we are to be pitied more than all men."

Think about it! If Christ has not been raised from the dead Christian faith is in vain. In other words, if Christ has not been resurrected from the dead, you can forget about Christianity because there is no hope for life after death. Without Jesus resurrection there can be no Christianity. For me these thoughts are more than depressing, they are as I stated above, devastating.

In concluding this chapter of scripture Paul adds the observation that if Christ has not been raised from the dead, he has suffered affliction for only human reasons. If there is no resurrection he says, "Let us eat and drink, for tomorrow we die" (verse 32).

I thank God that in the midst of his observations there jumps out a notation in verse 20 and following. "But Christ has indeed been raised from the dead, the first fruits of those who have fallen asleep...so in Christ all will be made alive." I read that and utter under my breath, "Thank God!" Yes, I believe in the resurrection of Jesus Christ.

But what is the evidence? There are many appearances of the resurrected Christ to people in the New Testament, first to the early disciples and to others who believed in Him and then to Paul on the road to Damascus.

In Matthew 28: verses 1 and following we find the report that the two Mary's went to the tomb early on Sunday morning, probably to anoint the body of Jesus. They found the tomb open. They were afraid and as they were running away they met Jesus. He told them to go tell his disciples. In that same chapter Matthew tells of the disciples going to Galilee to the mountain where Jesus had told them to go and there they saw and worshiped him but some still doubted.

Mark reports that Jesus met with the Eleven as they were eating. He rebuked them for their lake of faith and their refusal toe believe those who had already seen Him (Mark 16: 14)

Luke reports that Jesus met with two men who were walking to Emmaus. They were discussing the events around the crucifixion when Jesus joined the conversation. They did not at first recognize Him until He was leaving them (Luke 24). He again met with the Eleven and they recognized Him (Luke 24: 16 and following).

John reports (John 20) that Jesus came into the closed room where the disciples were meeting. He greeted them with "Peace be with you." He again met with the disciples when they were fishing the next morning and told them where to cast their net to catch more fish. They did and He shared fish with them.

Paul reports that Jesus appeared to Peter and the twelve and after that to more than five hundred at one time. He later appeared to James and all the apostles then, Paul says, "He appeared to me as one abnormally born." He was born after the experiences of the other disciples and encountered the resurrected "Christ on the road to Damascus.

There are thousands of others over the years who have reported encounters with the resurrected Jesus. I personally know of one. I know I have already shared this but it impacted my life so much I want to repeat it and hope it sticks with readers. He was the friend who was dying with a painful blood disease. I went to see him one Saturday morning and found him, not in bed as he had been but standing in the bathroom shaving. I expressed surprise but he said, "Jesus came to me last night and told me I was healed. I am feeling fine."

As indicated earlier he died a short time later. I still believe that he either saw Jesus or had a vision of Jesus that prepared him for his death.

I have never seen Jesus but in August of 1964 I was awakened in the middle of the night with a strong experience of an awareness of His presence. I was in my bed alone and became aware of someone in the room. I raised up and spoke to the one I presumed to be my wife. There was no one there. That may not seem like much to some but the experience impacted my life in ways that I will never forget.

Is he alive? All the above testimonies says yes and so does the changed lives of thousands of others over the years and the continued existence of the church that continues to proclaim faith in the resurrected Christ.

I believe He is alive and I believed that before reviewing the testimonies about His presence in the lives of so many people. I believe and trust that He is the resurrected Lord and lives in our lives today.

There is personal evidence supporting belief in a resurrected Jesus. That faith enables me to find comfort for the loss of loved ones and friends.

In spite of my continued failures over the years my faith in a resurrected Lord has impacted my values. When I experience anxiety about the future I spend time talking to Him and my anxiety is usually reduced.

As I have indicated earlier I know that I did things in my years as a pastor that I could not or would not have done if I had not believed in His living presence. Some of those things include leading the church to become open to integration. This took place in the late sixties.

We voted to have an equal number of men and women serving as deacons and opened the door for women to be ordained and preach when others in our denomination were not permitting this to happen. We were able to ordain a young woman who believed she was called to be a chaplain. Churches in her state refused to ordain her because she was a woman. We ordained her and several years later she wrote a letter of thanks to the church and said she was still serving as a chaplain.

The list goes on. We recognized that we should accept divorced people to serve in the church. We accepted members who had not been baptized by Baptists and some who had not been immersed at all. Communion was open to all who attended church. We stocked two benevolent pantries and fed literally hundreds of people from them.

These and many others things happened because of our faith in a resurrected Lord. Yes, I believe in the resurrection of Jesus.

Conclusion: I have attempted to deal with several frequently asked questions about God's existence and religious faith in general. After presented several philosophical and many practical answers the questions still remain. I have clearly stated that we will never in this lifetime get all the answers but there is still nothing remiss about asking.

After my attempts to deal with as many questions as I could think of and then doing the best I could to answer them, I still have questions.

Bibliography

Barclay, William, "The Letters of John," Westminster Press, Louisville, KY, 1975

Bonhoeffer, Dietrich, "The Cost of Discipleship, "Macmilian Company, NY, NY 1968

Collins, Francis S., "Belief: the reason for faith, Harper Collins, New York, NY, 2010

Frankl, Viktor, "Man's Search for Meaning," Simon & Schuster, NY, NY, 1972

Porter, Katherine, "Ship of Fools," Little, Brown Co, Boston, 1962

Stanley, Andy, "Irresistible," Zondervan, Grand Rapids, Mich. 2018

The Arbinger Institute, "The Anatomy of Peace," Berrett-Koehler Pub., San Francisco, 2006

Wyatt, Karen, "What Really Matters." Sunroom Studios< Silverthrone, CO, 2011